Luís Stabile

TINY DIVAS

Coloring Book Halloween Edition

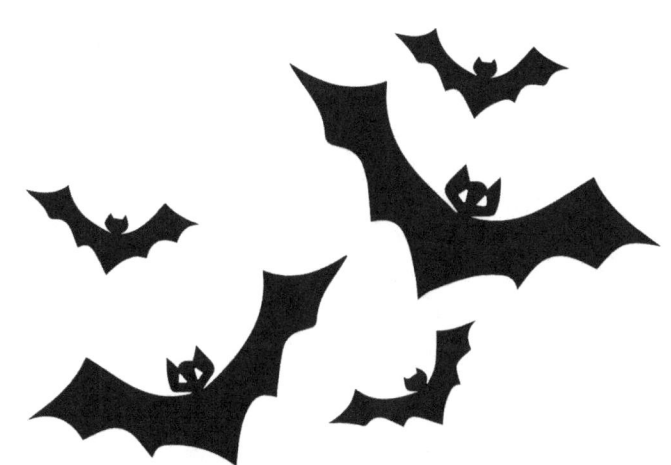

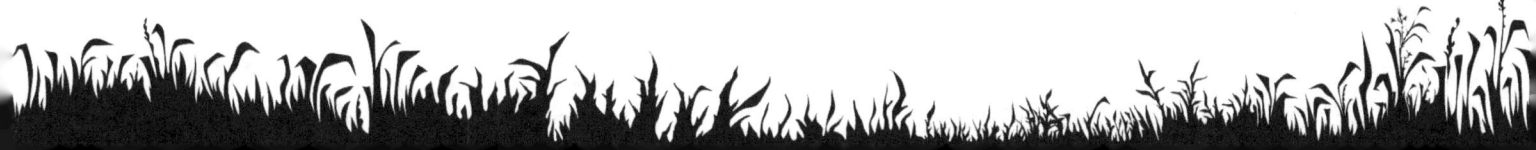

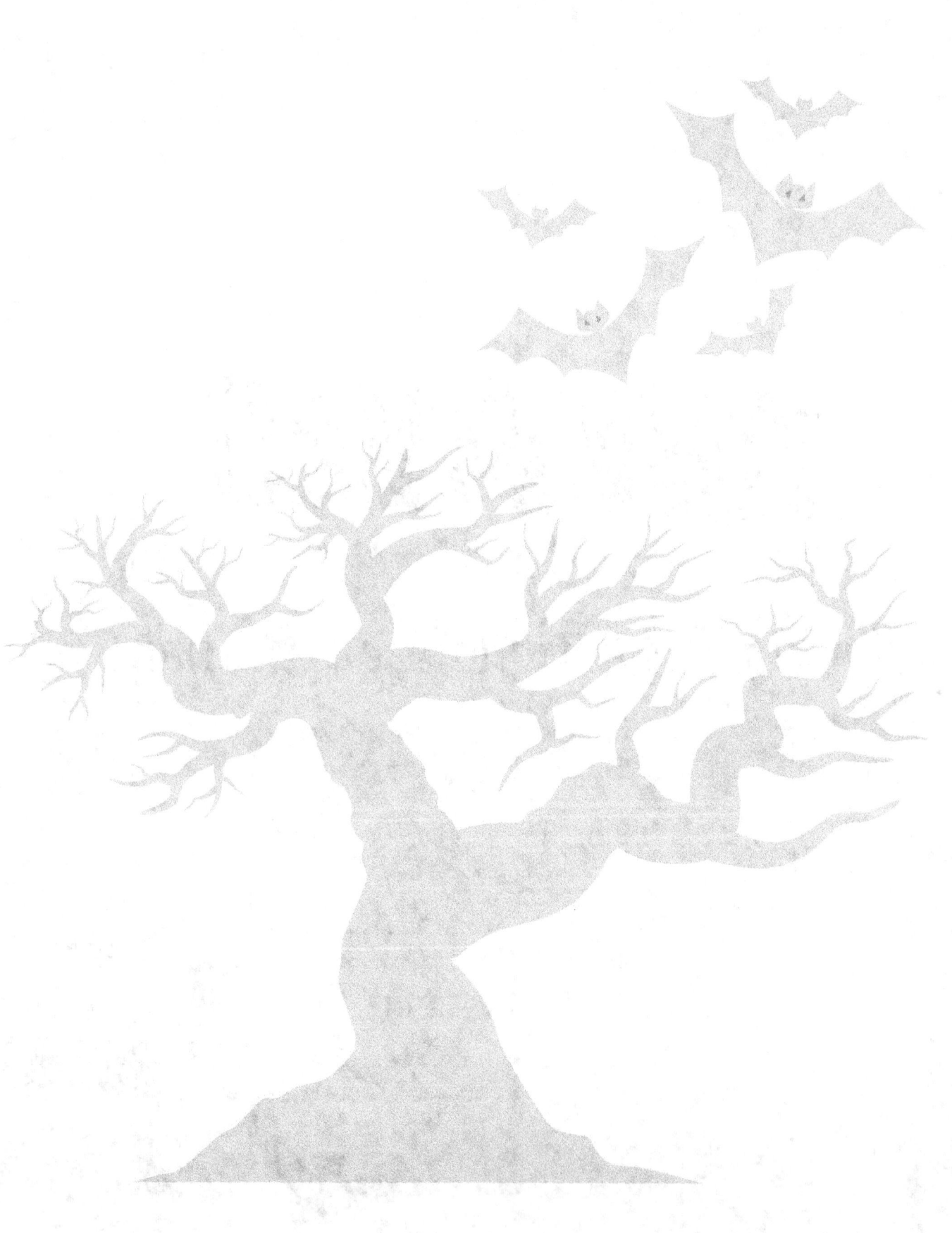

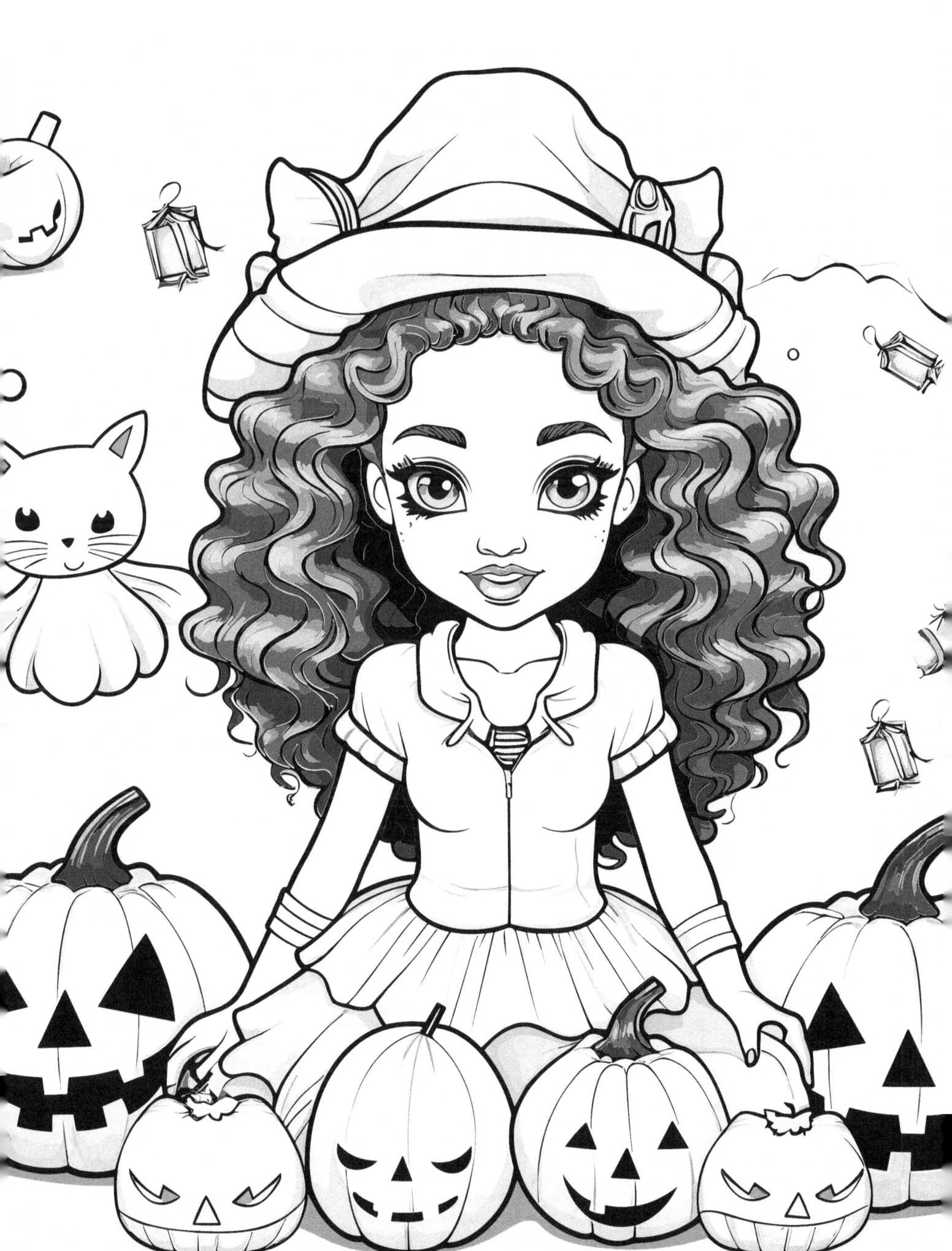

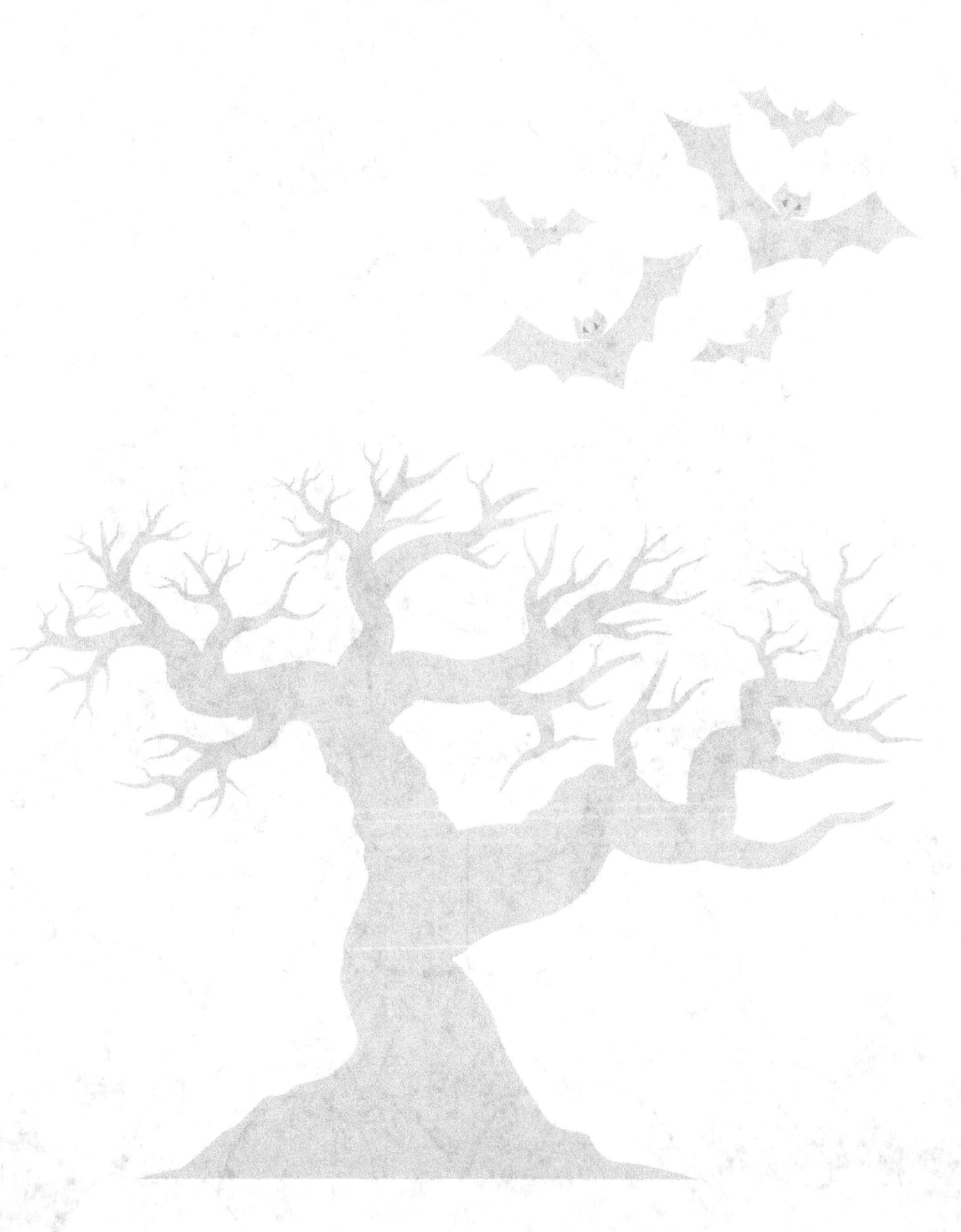

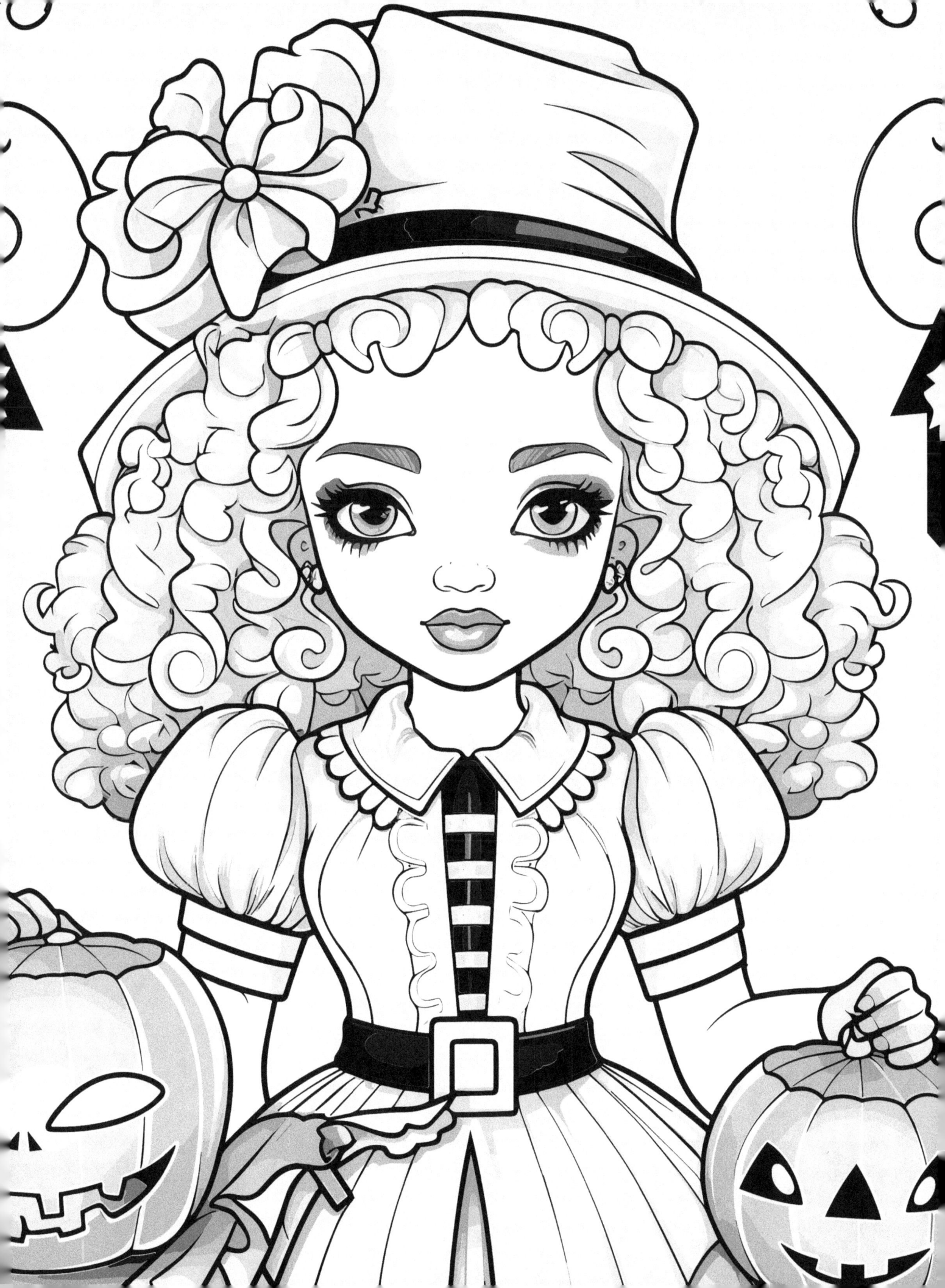

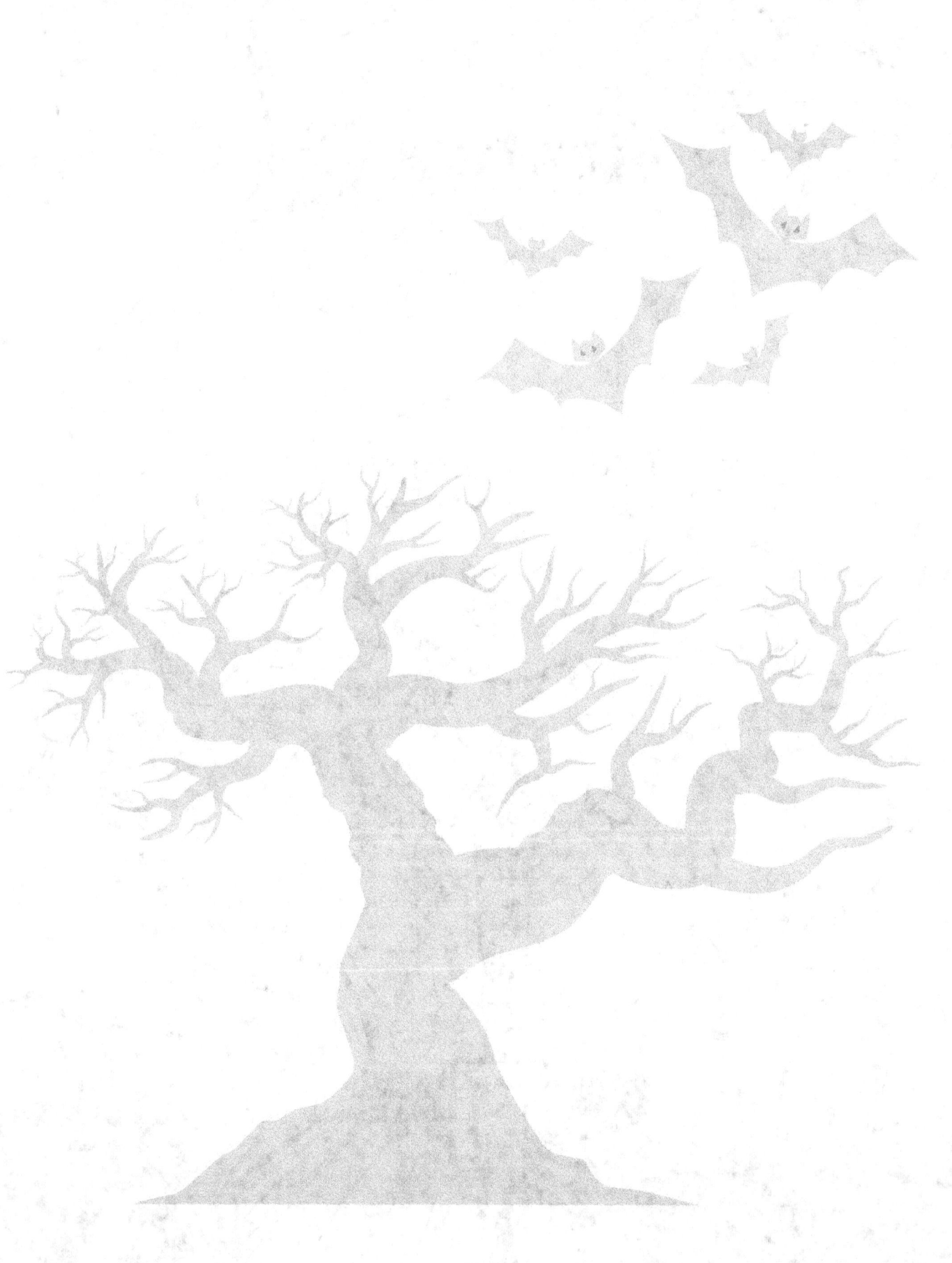

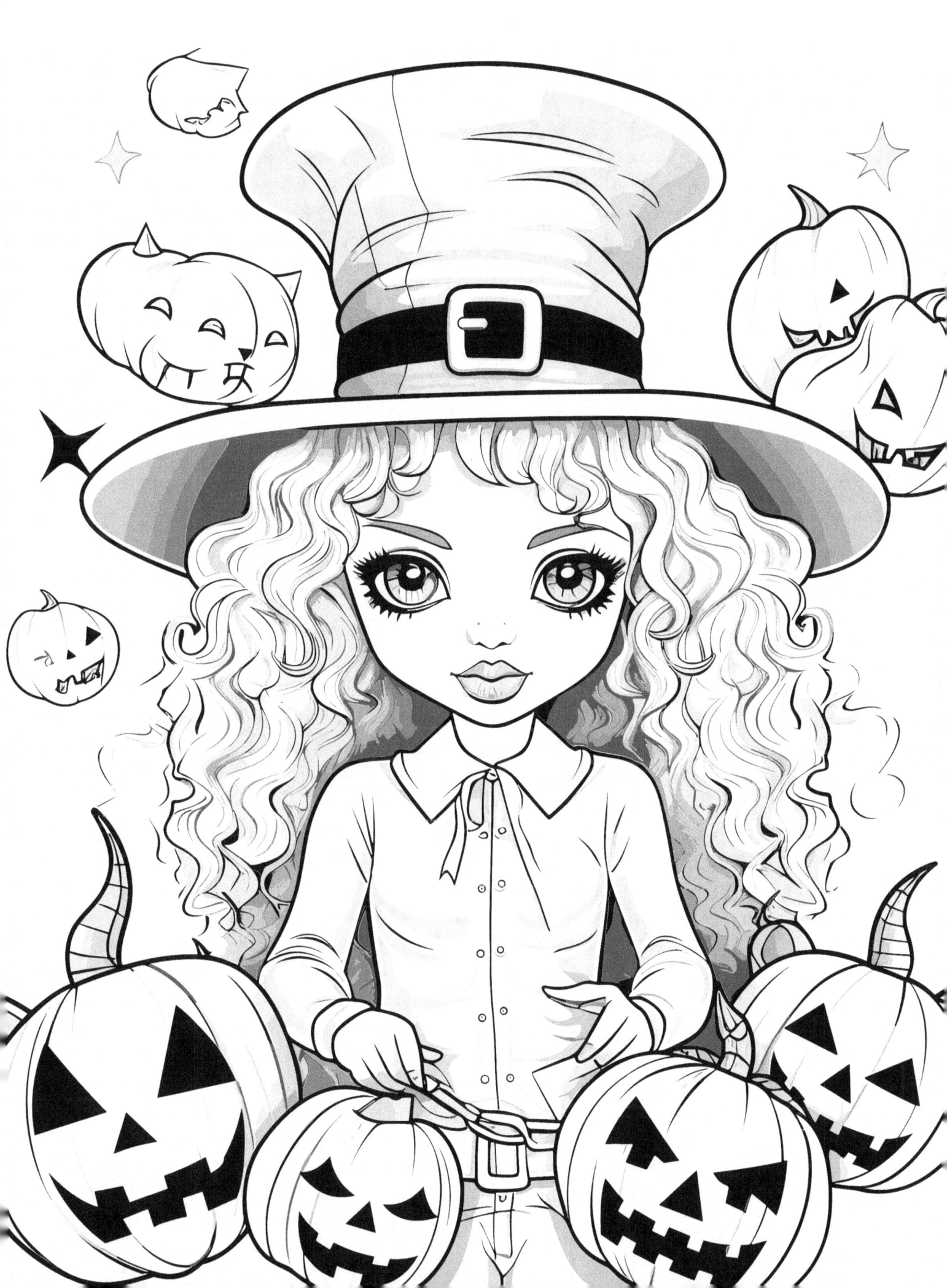

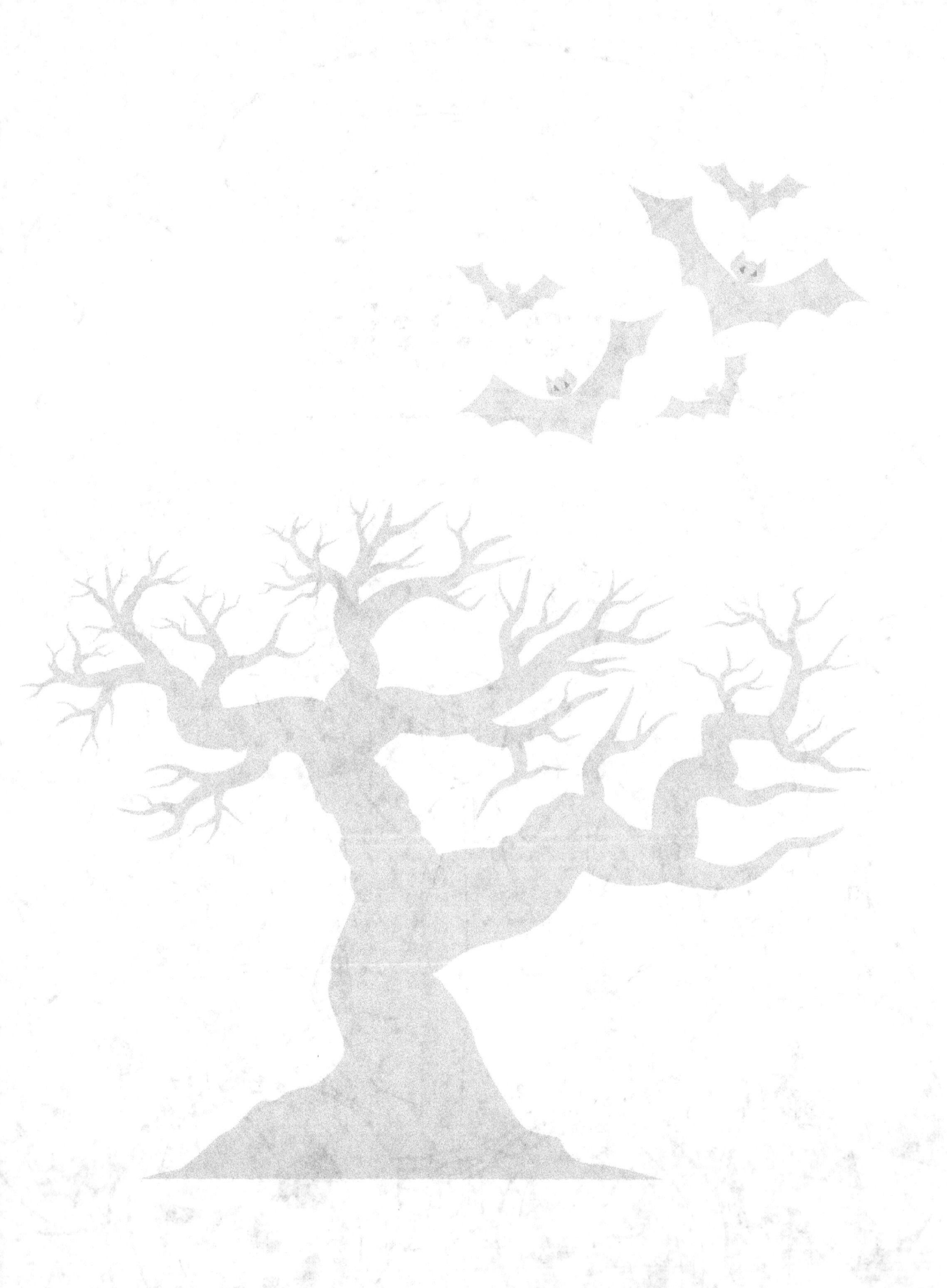

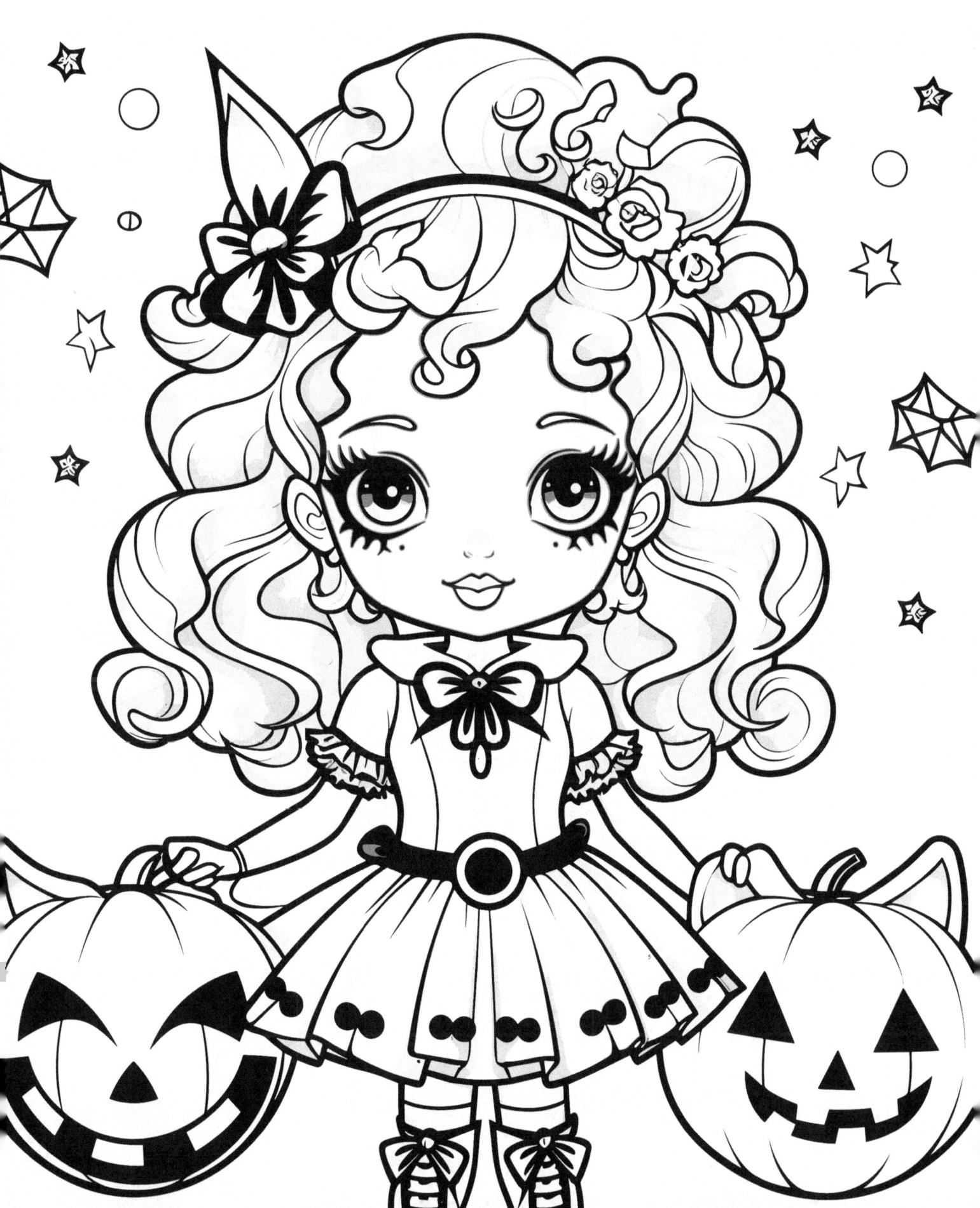

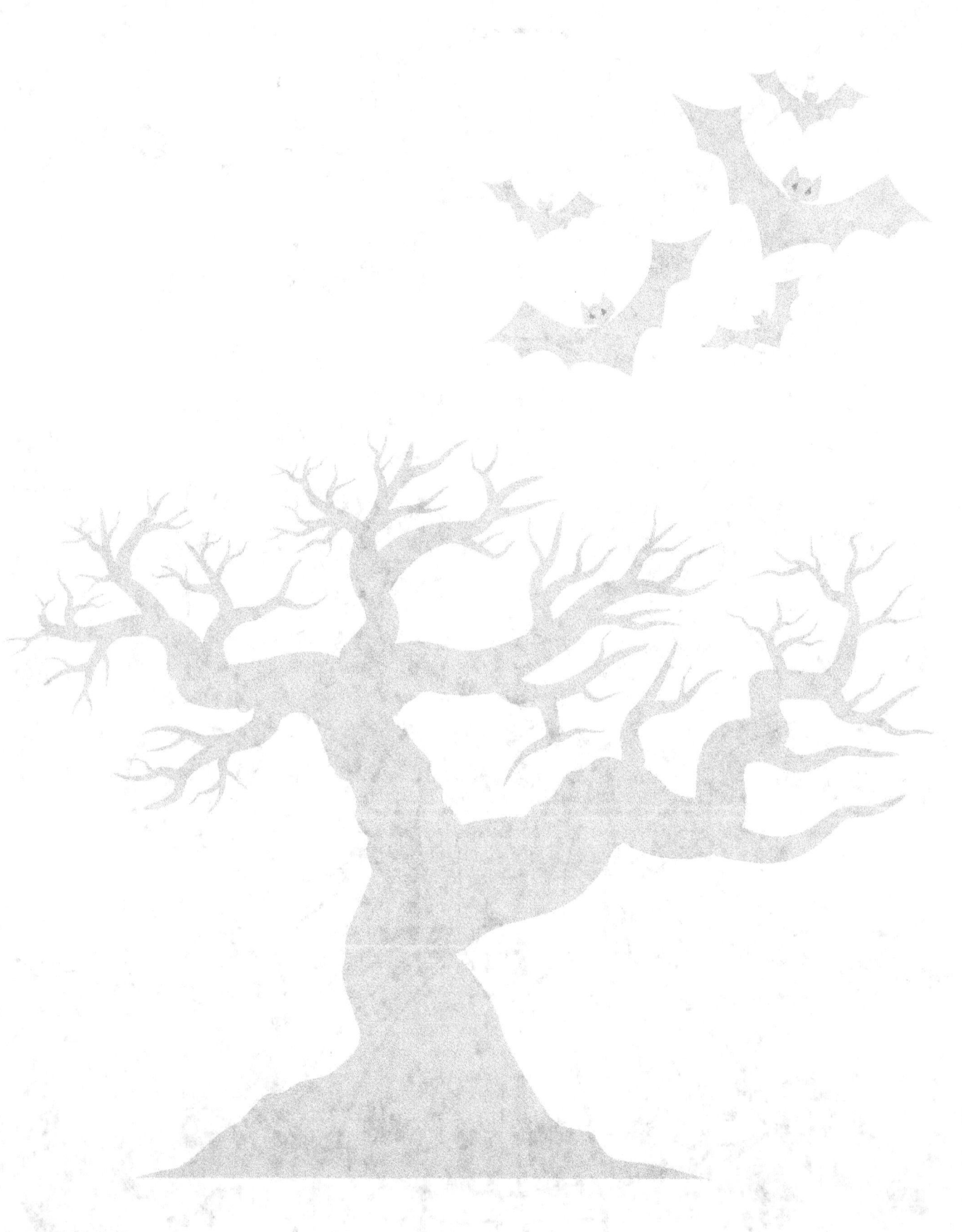

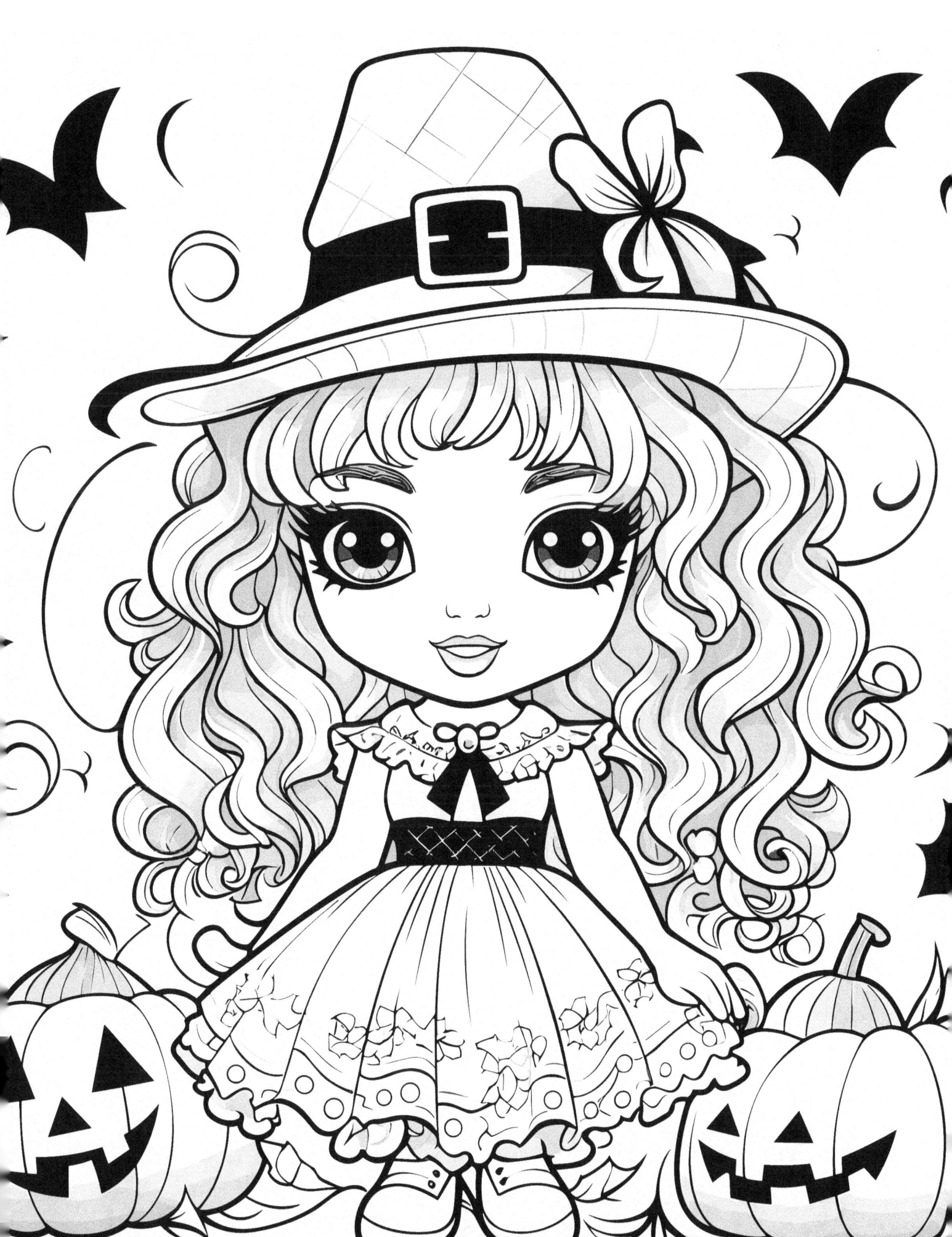

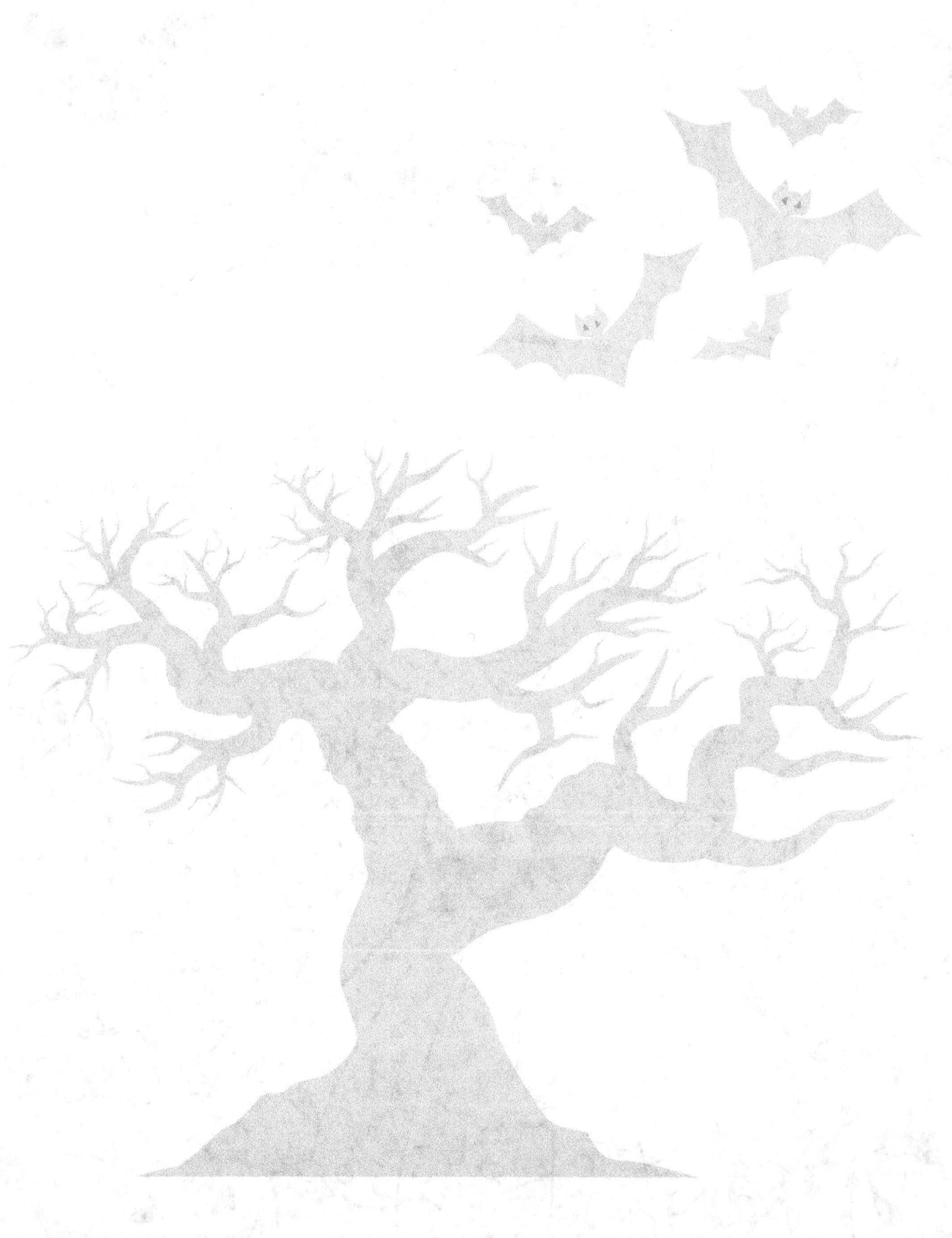

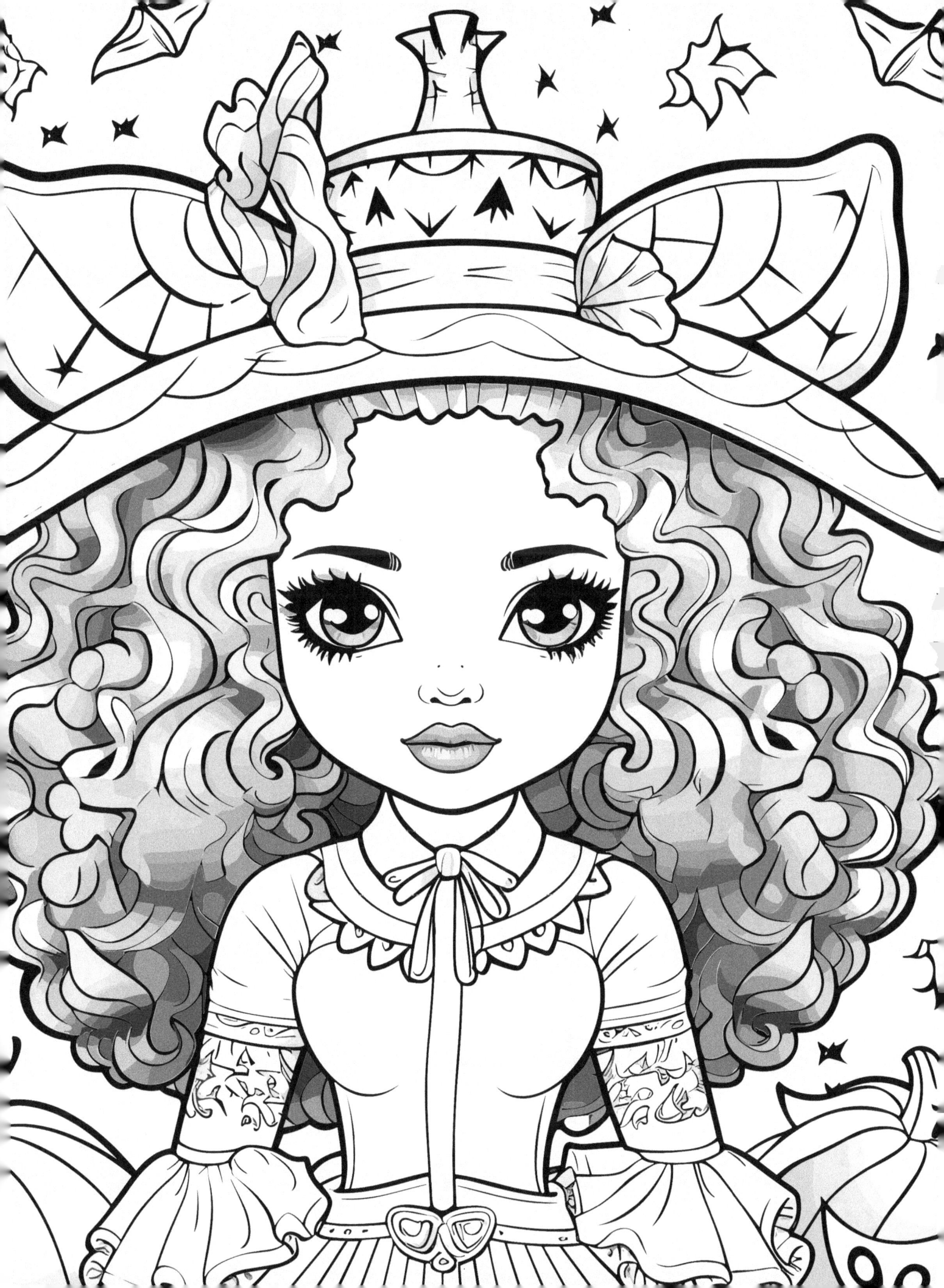

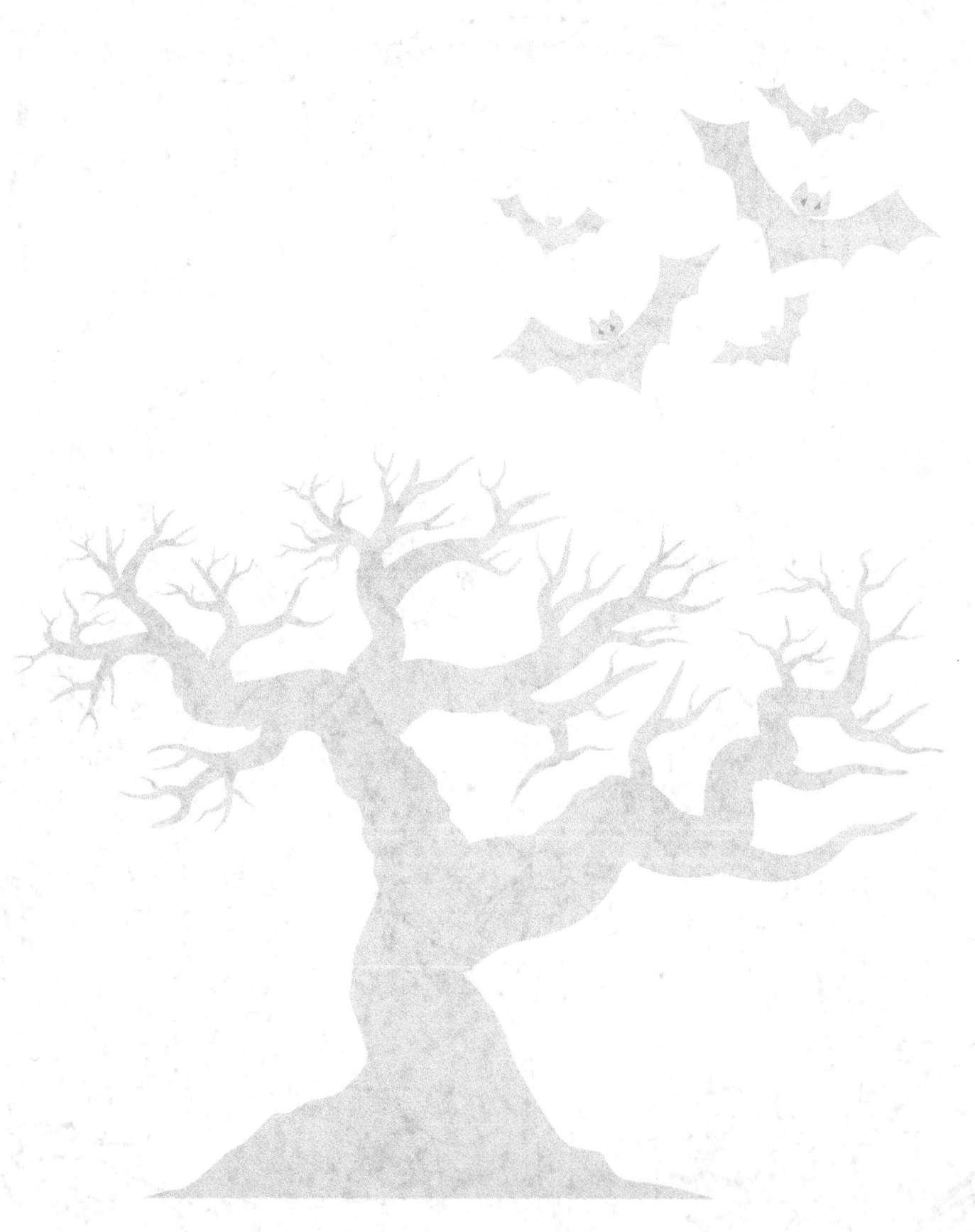

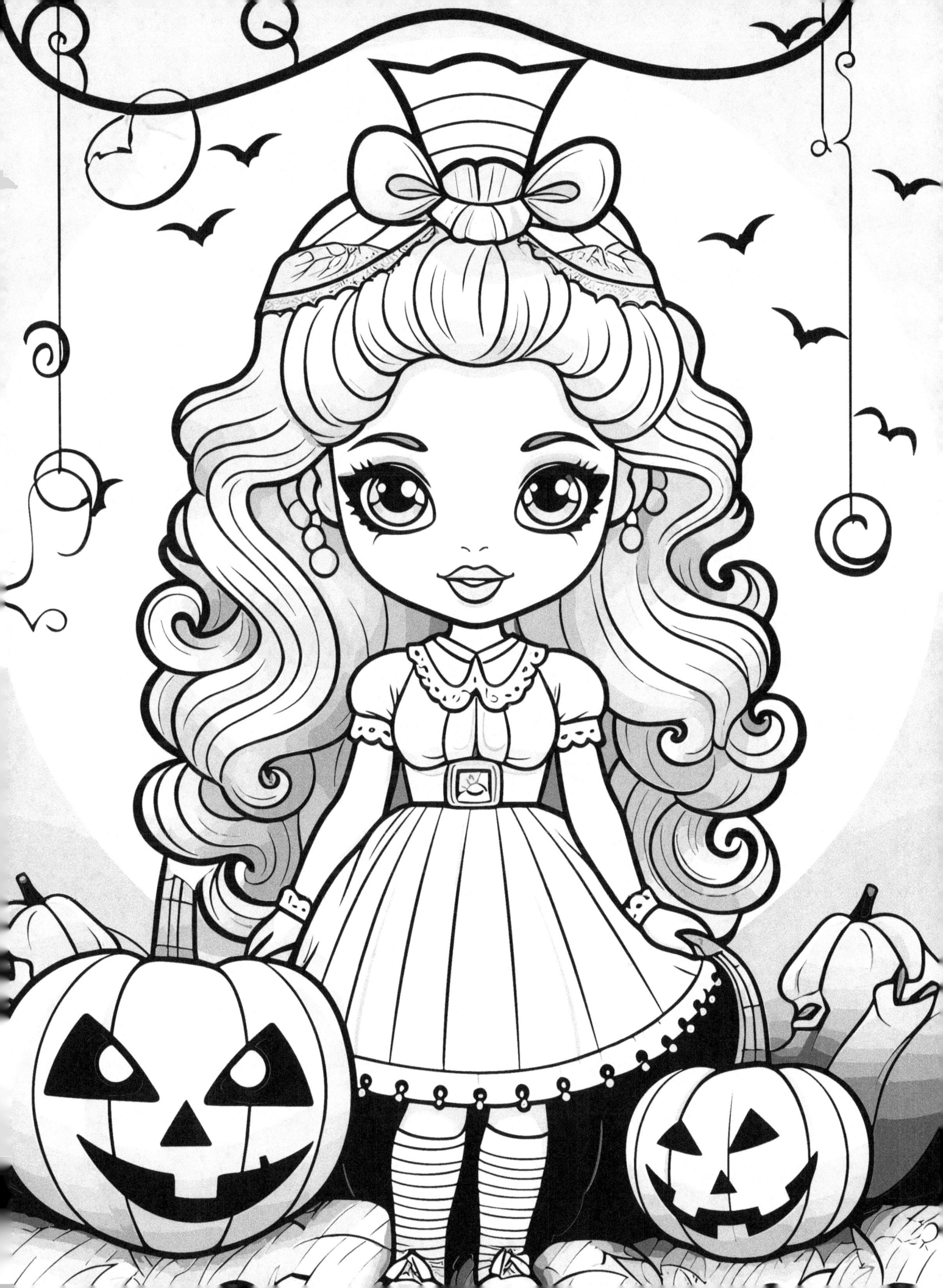

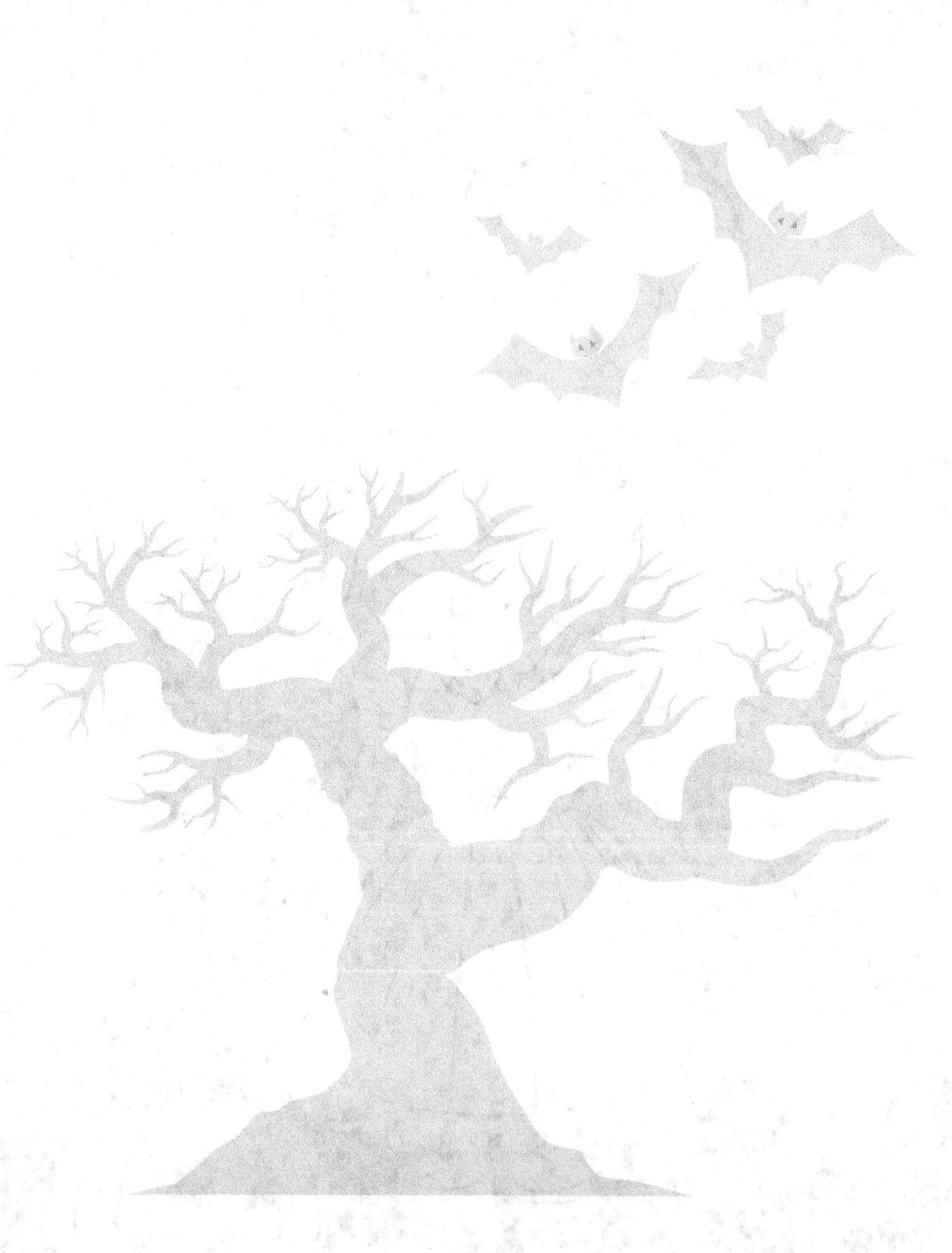

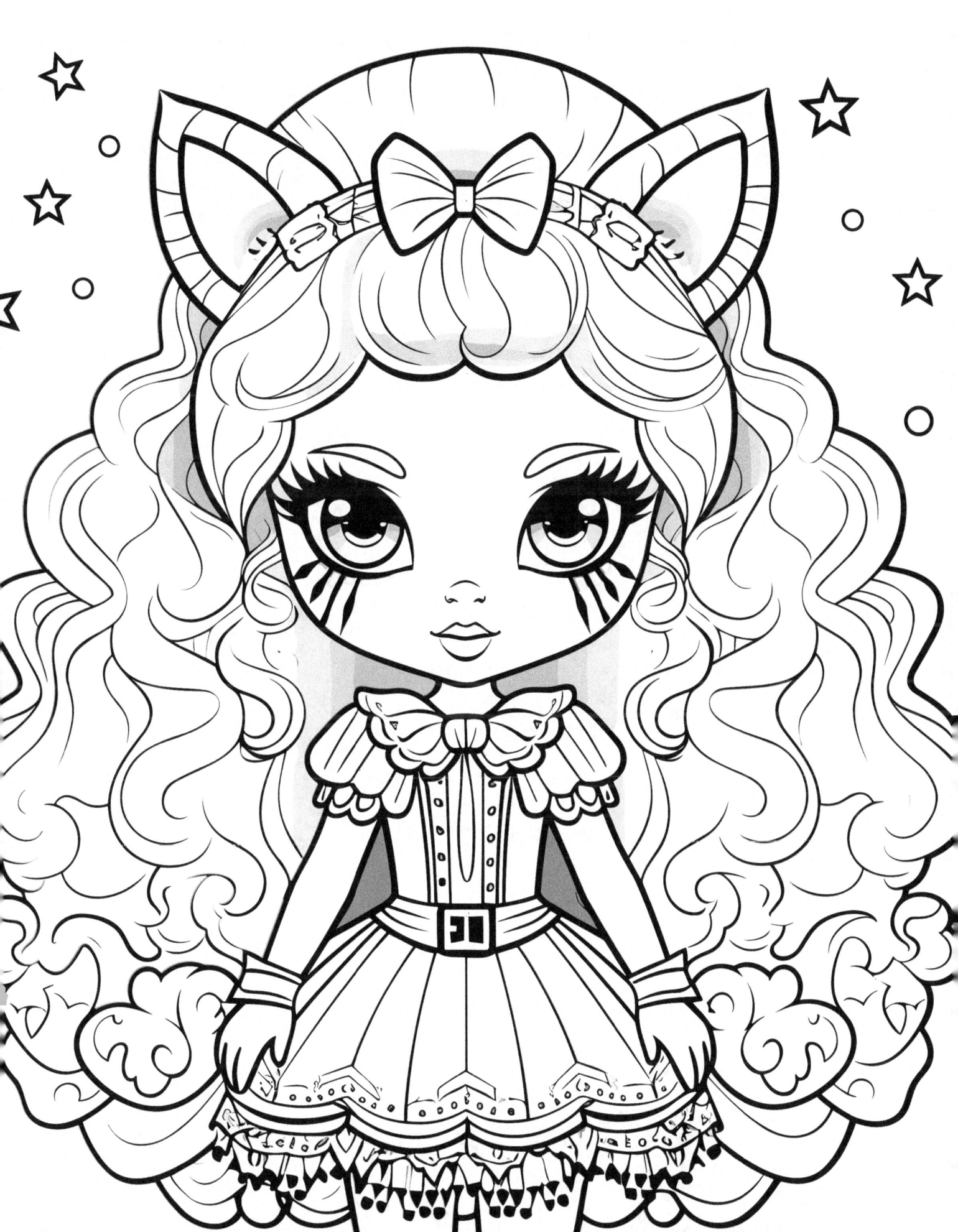

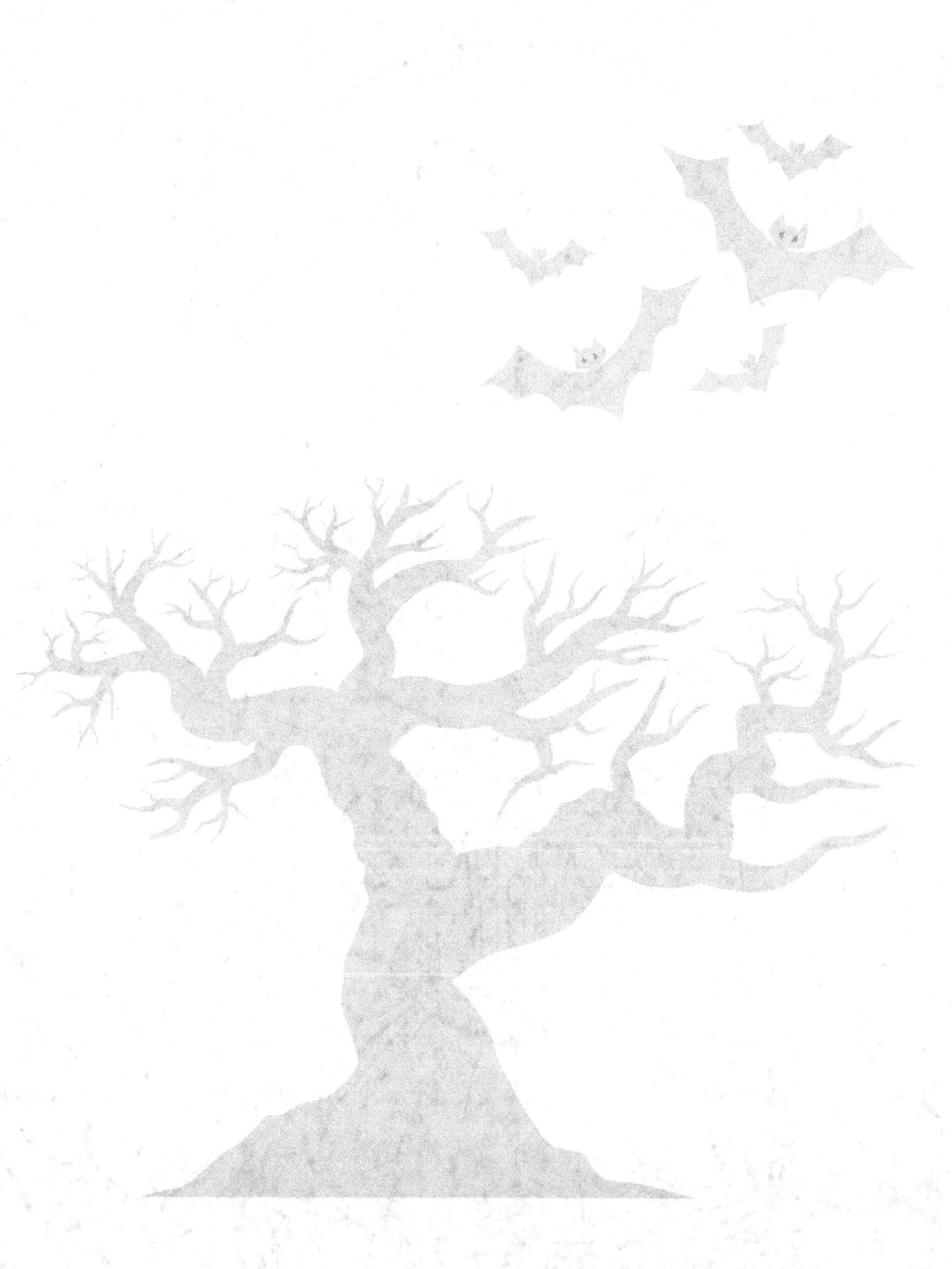

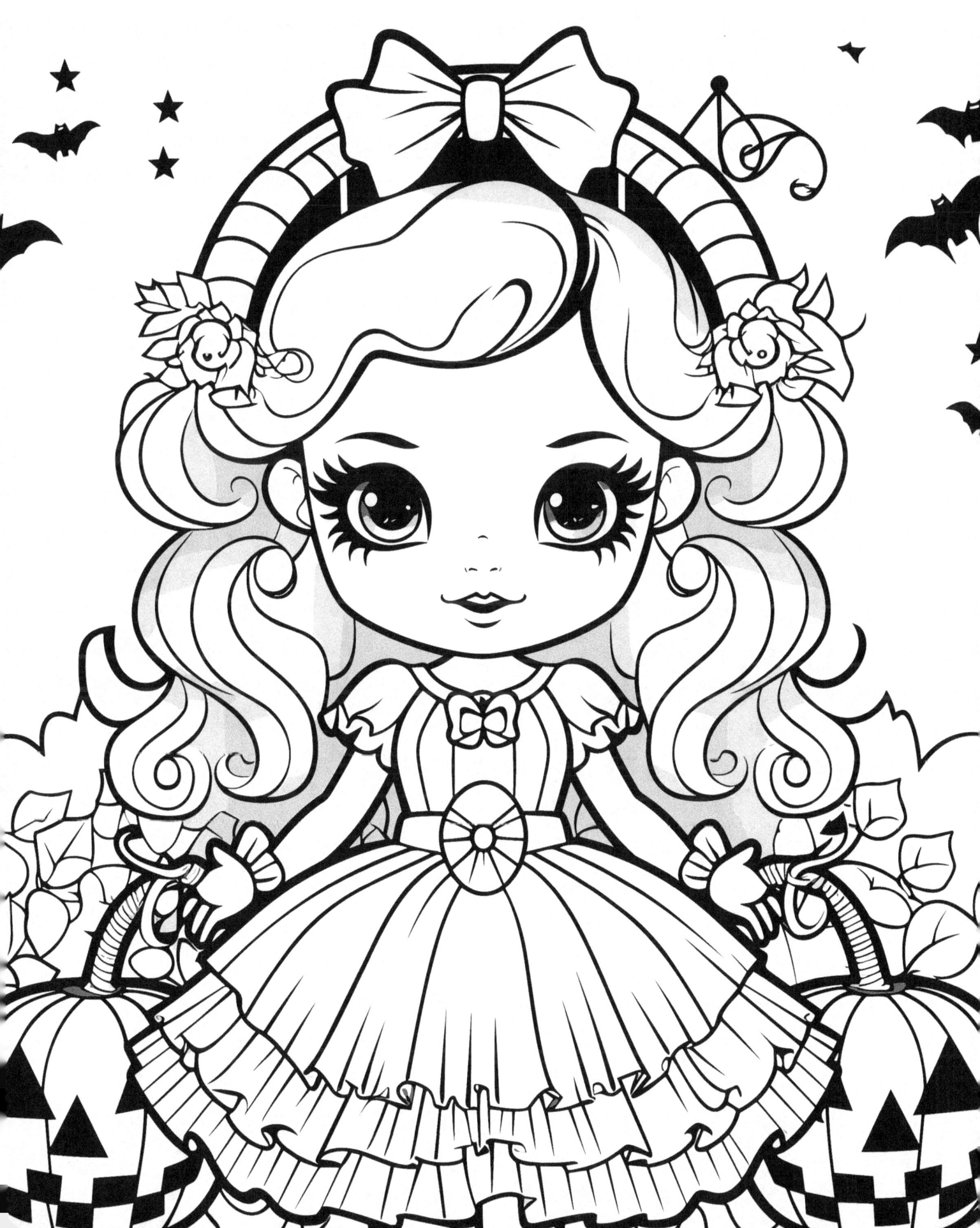

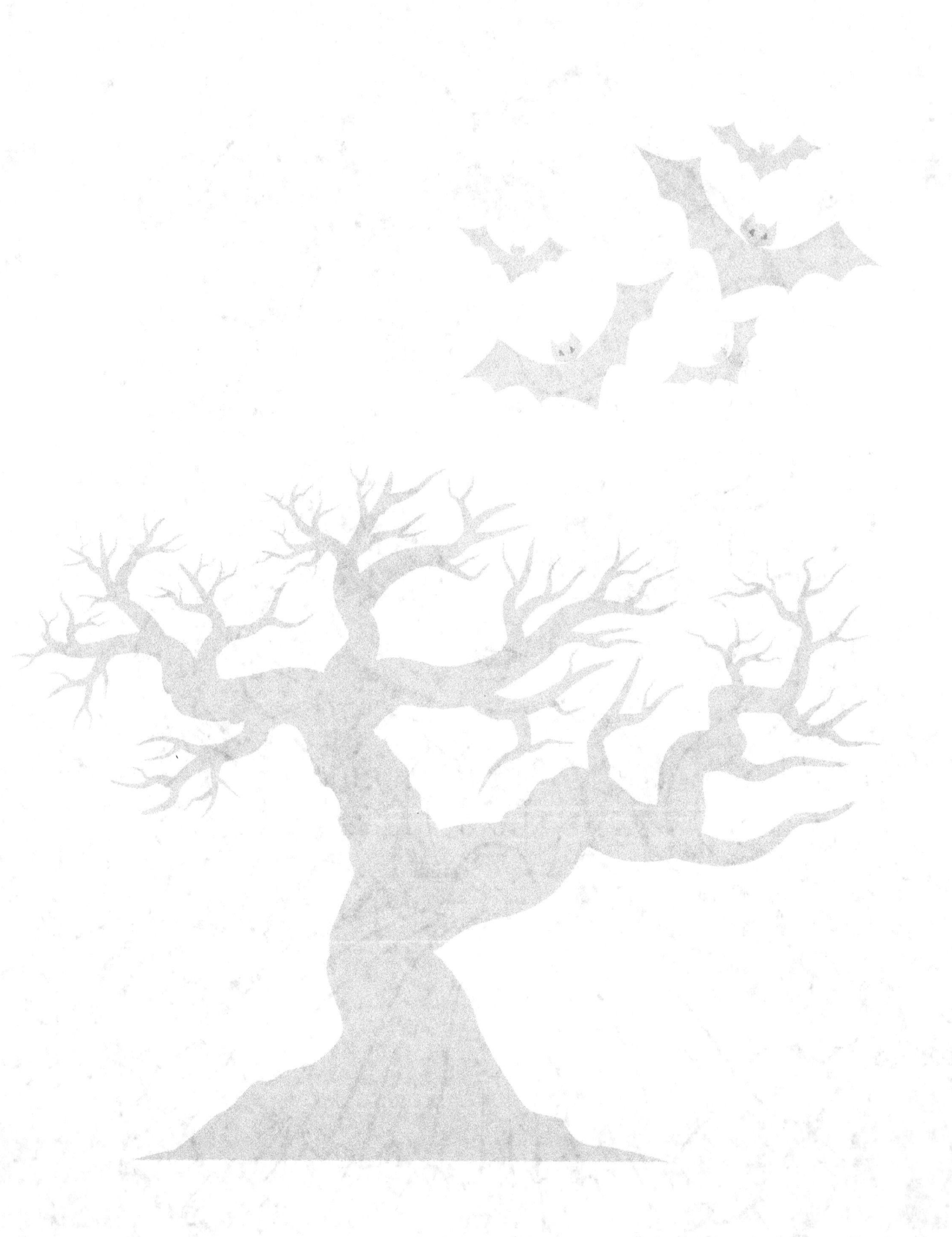

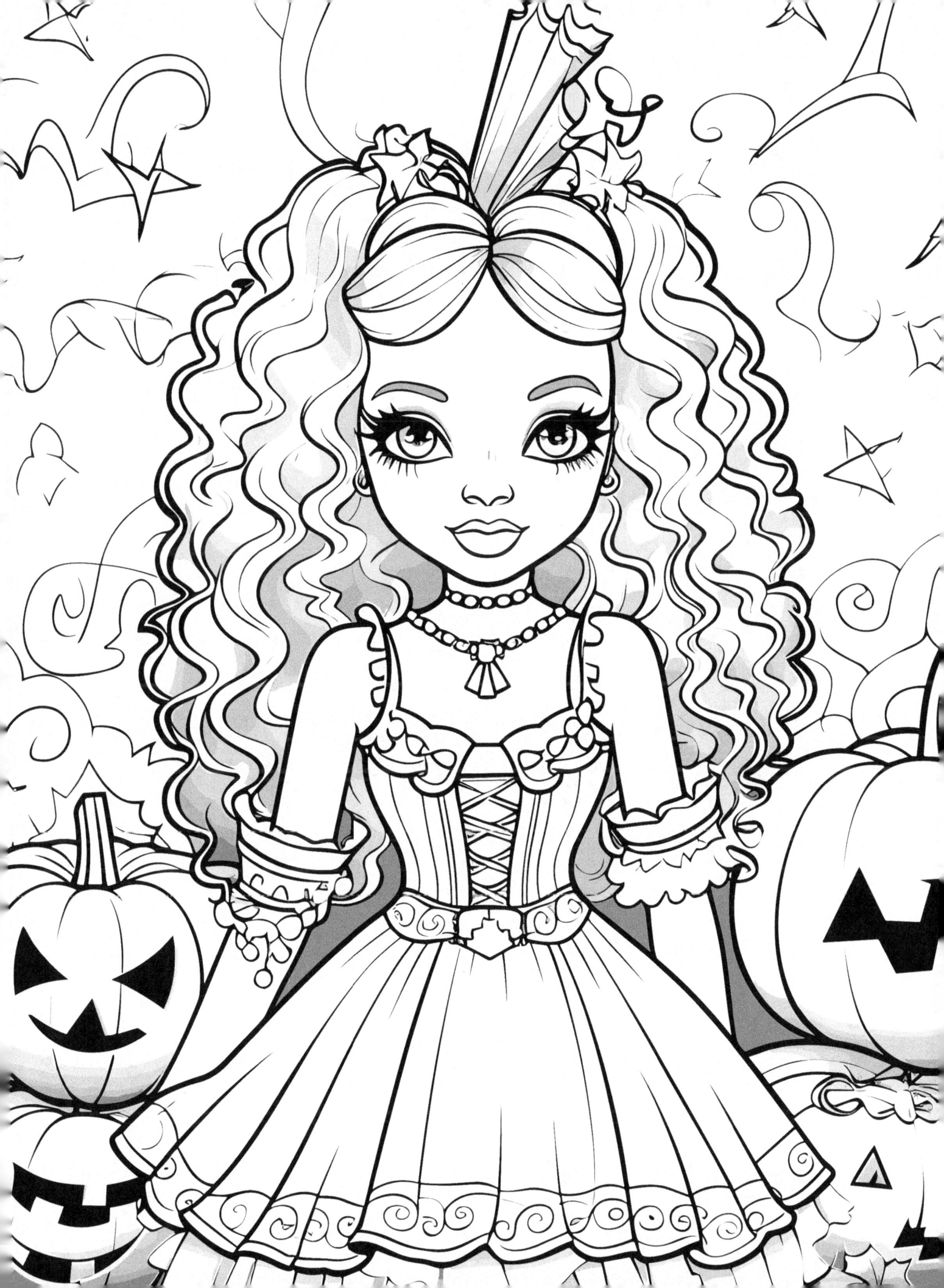

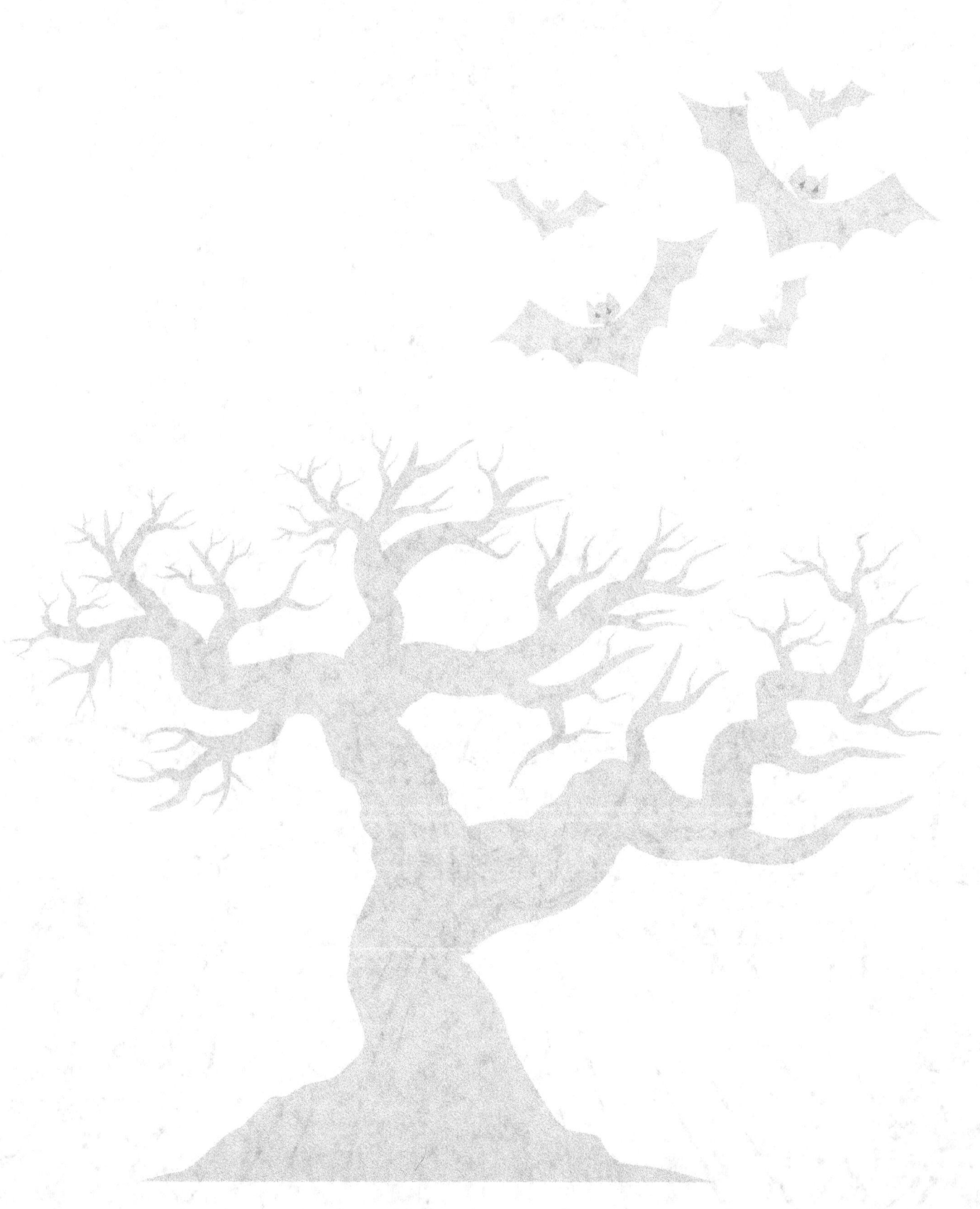

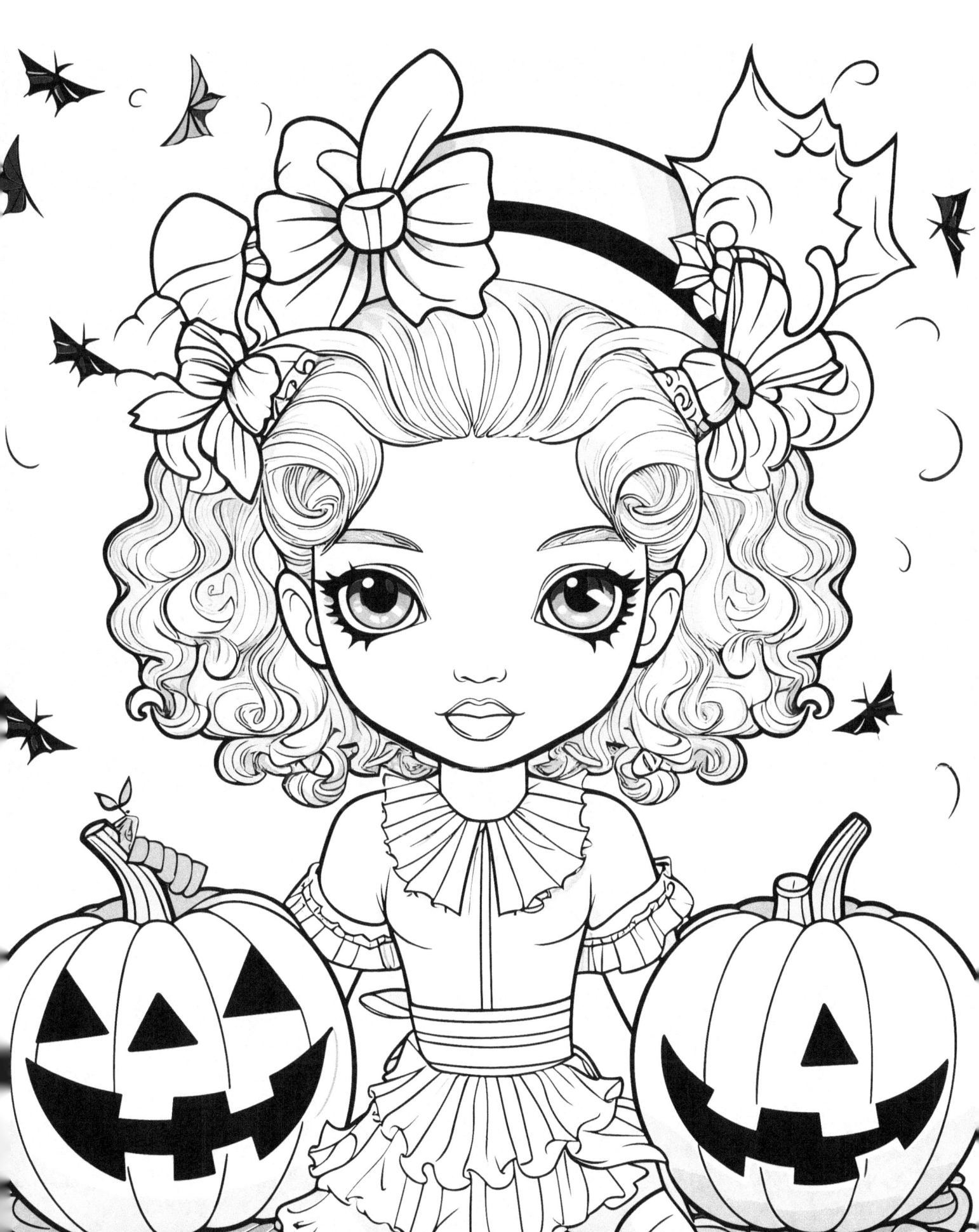

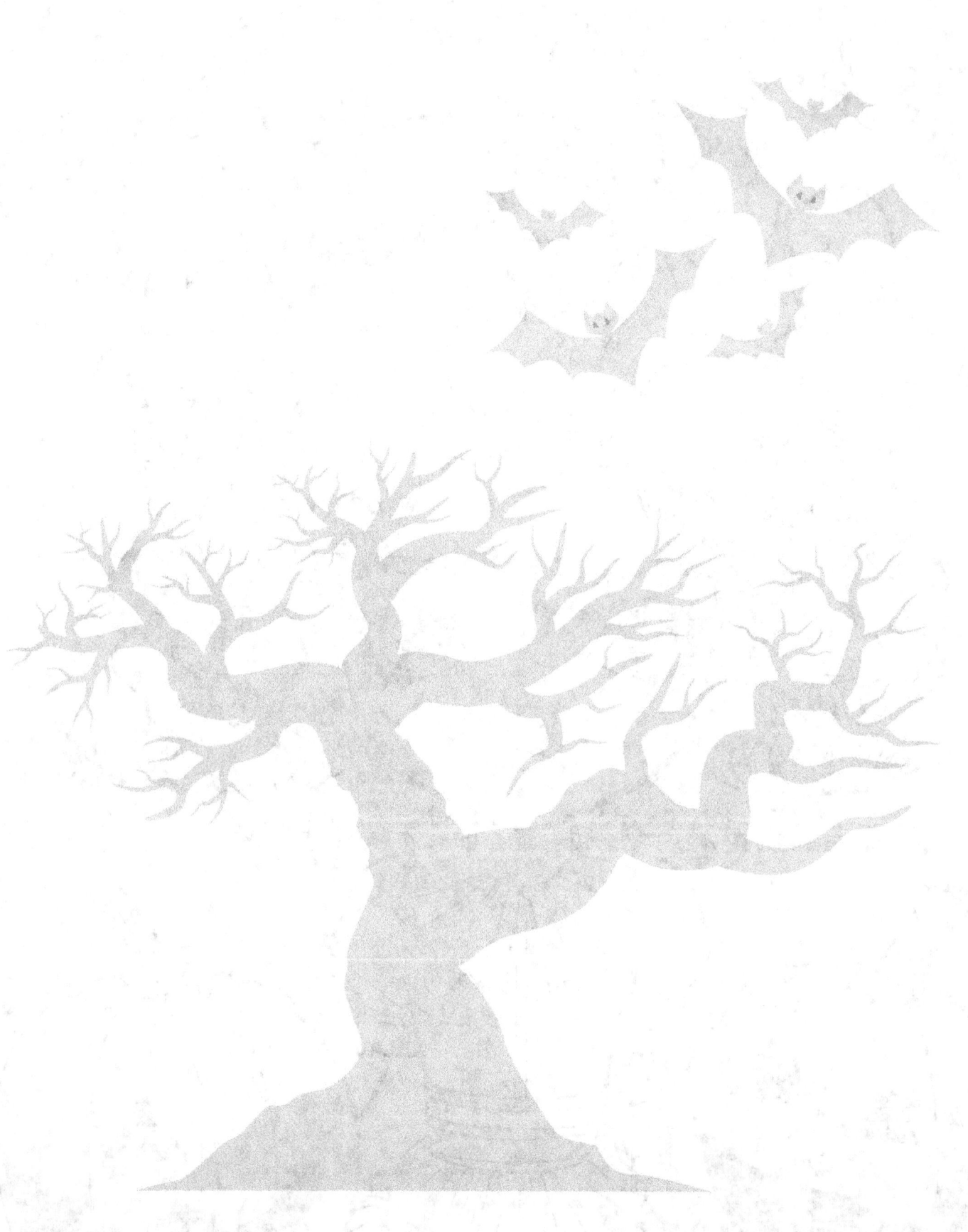

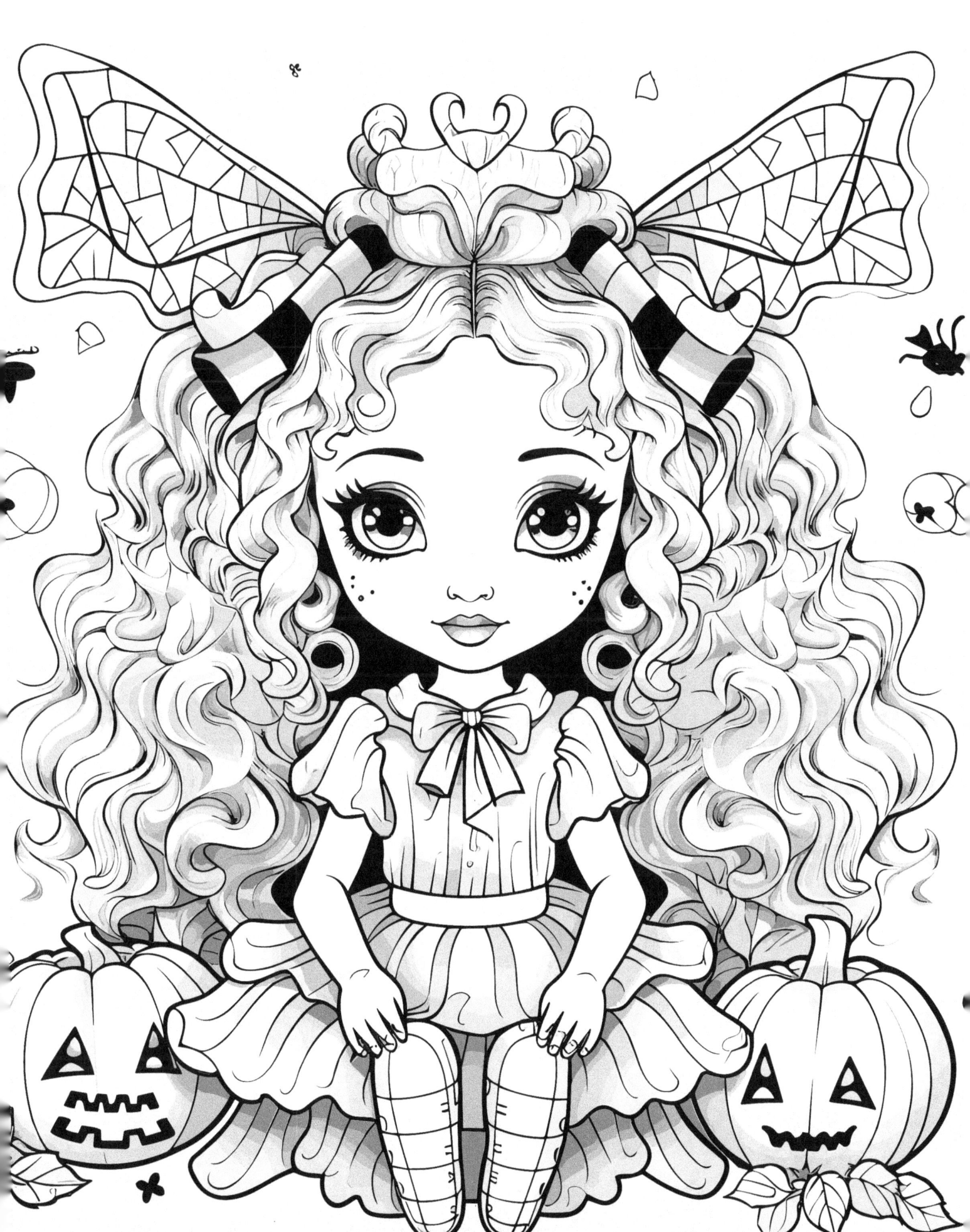

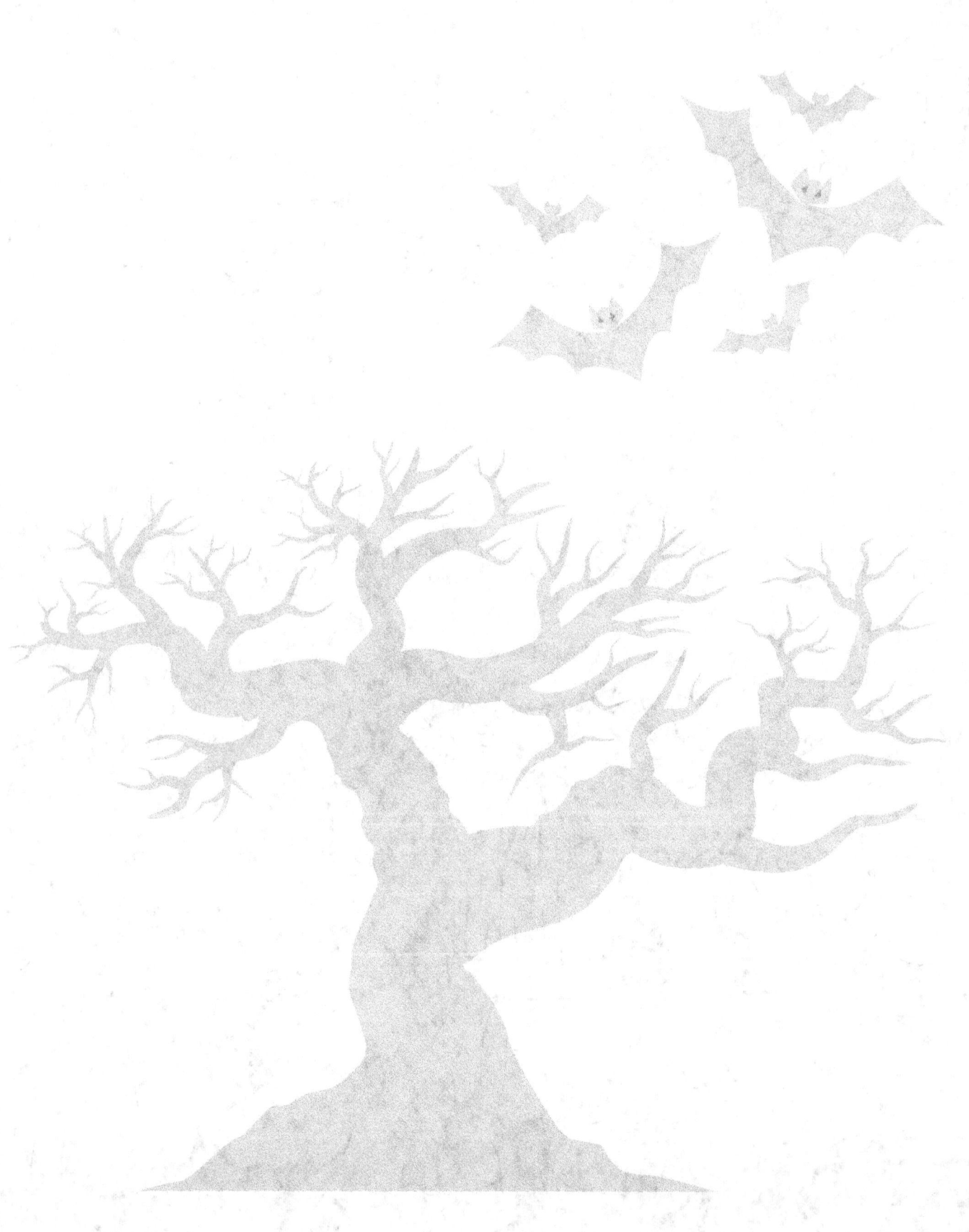

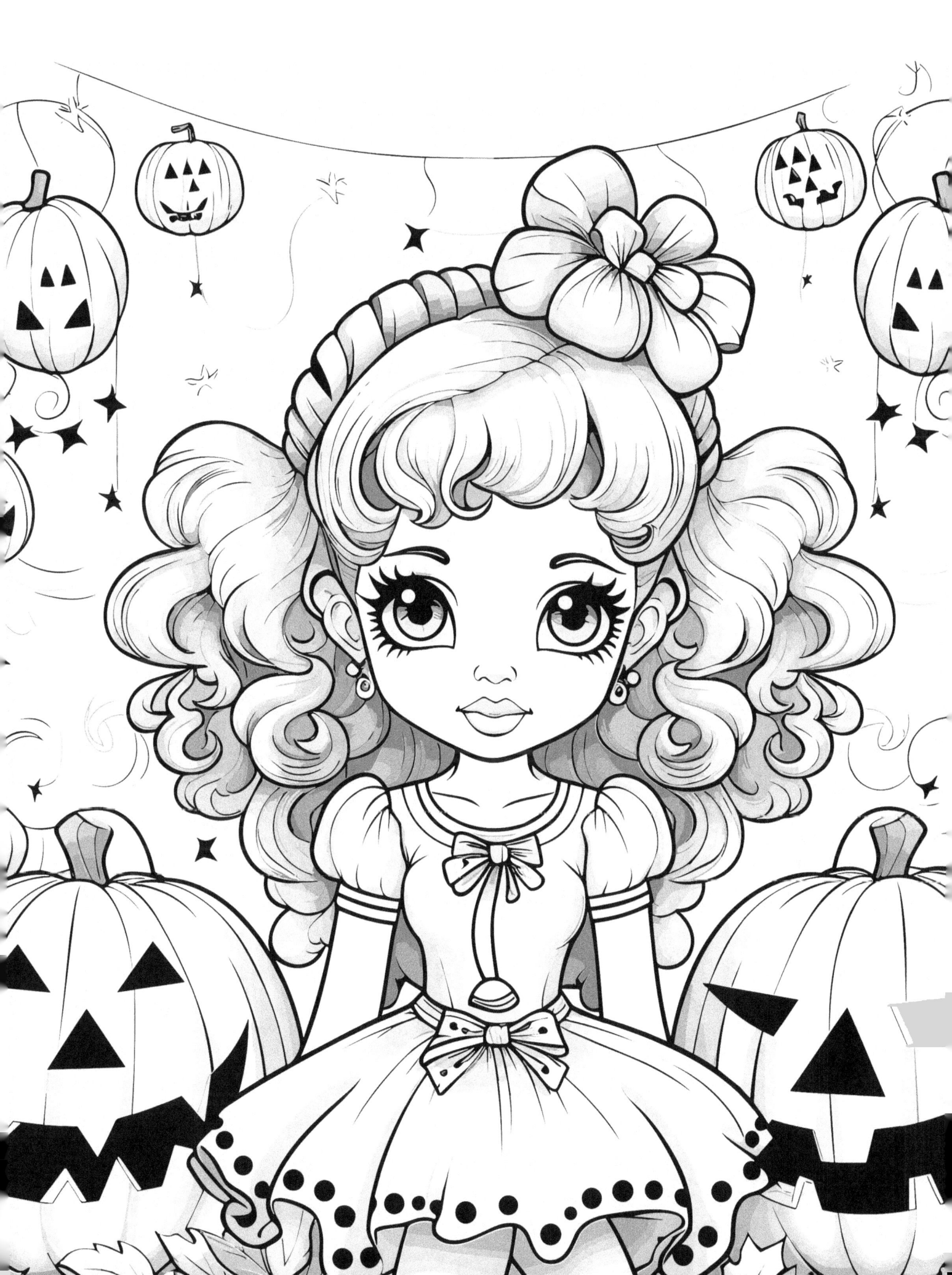

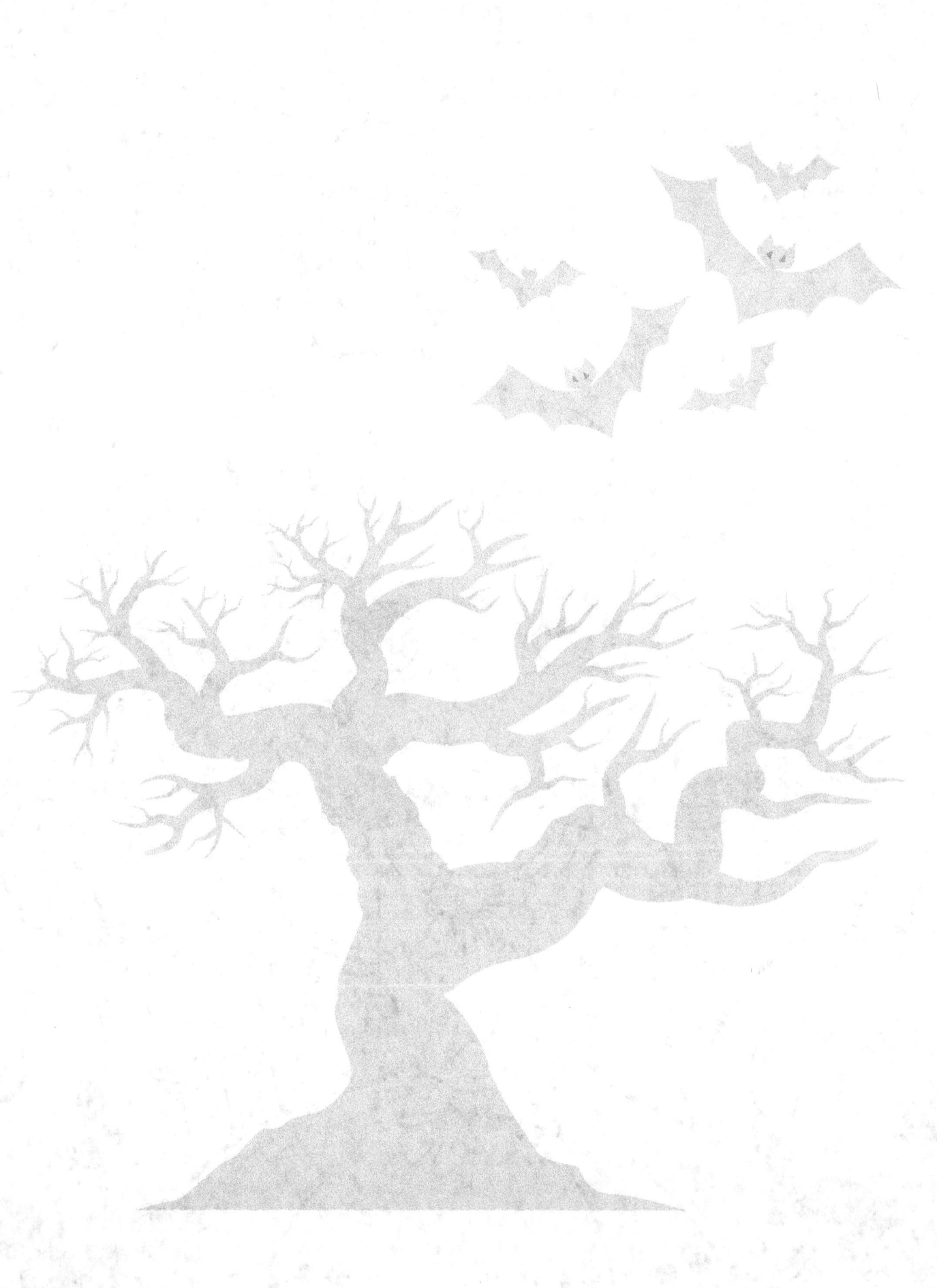

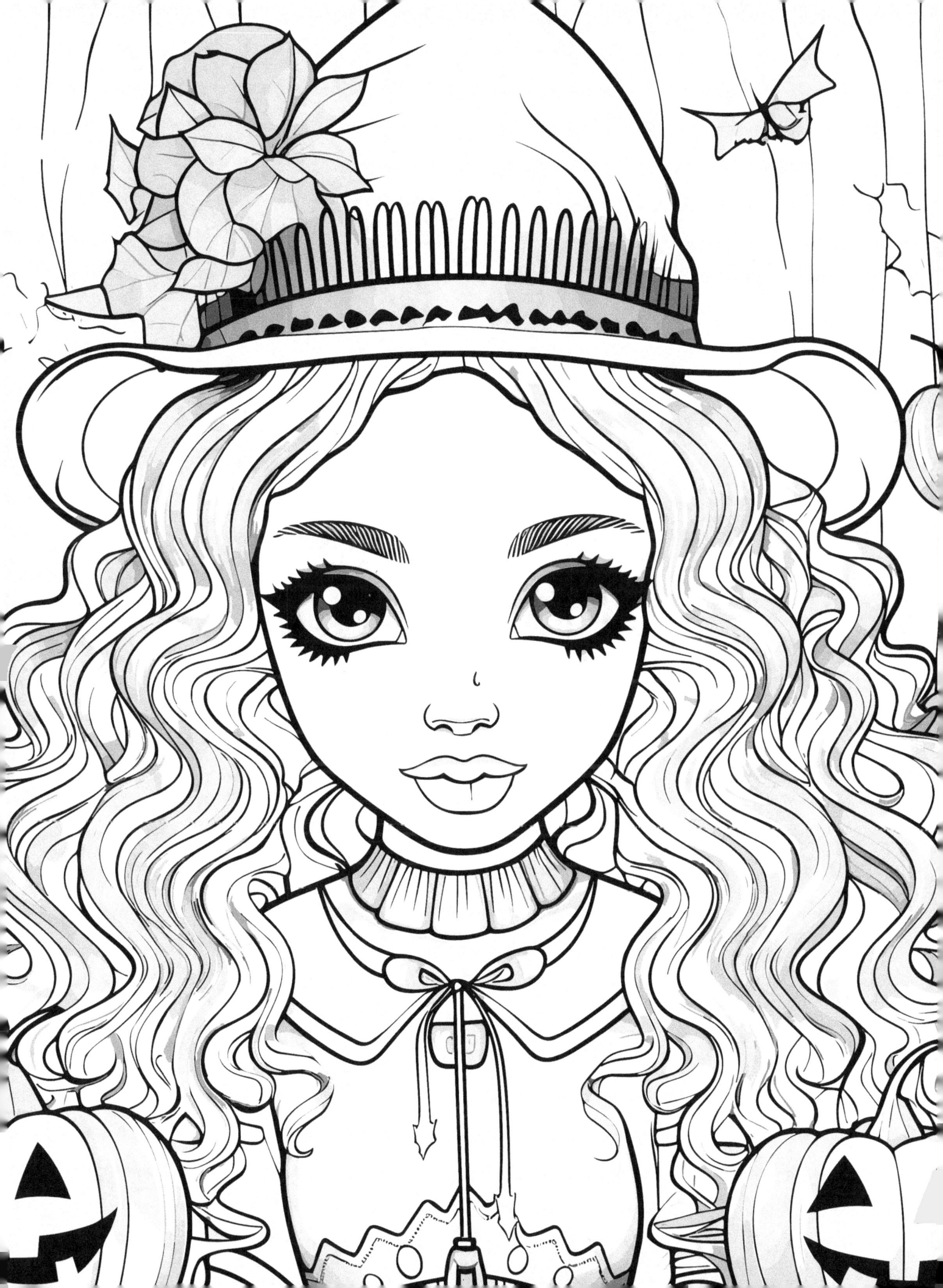

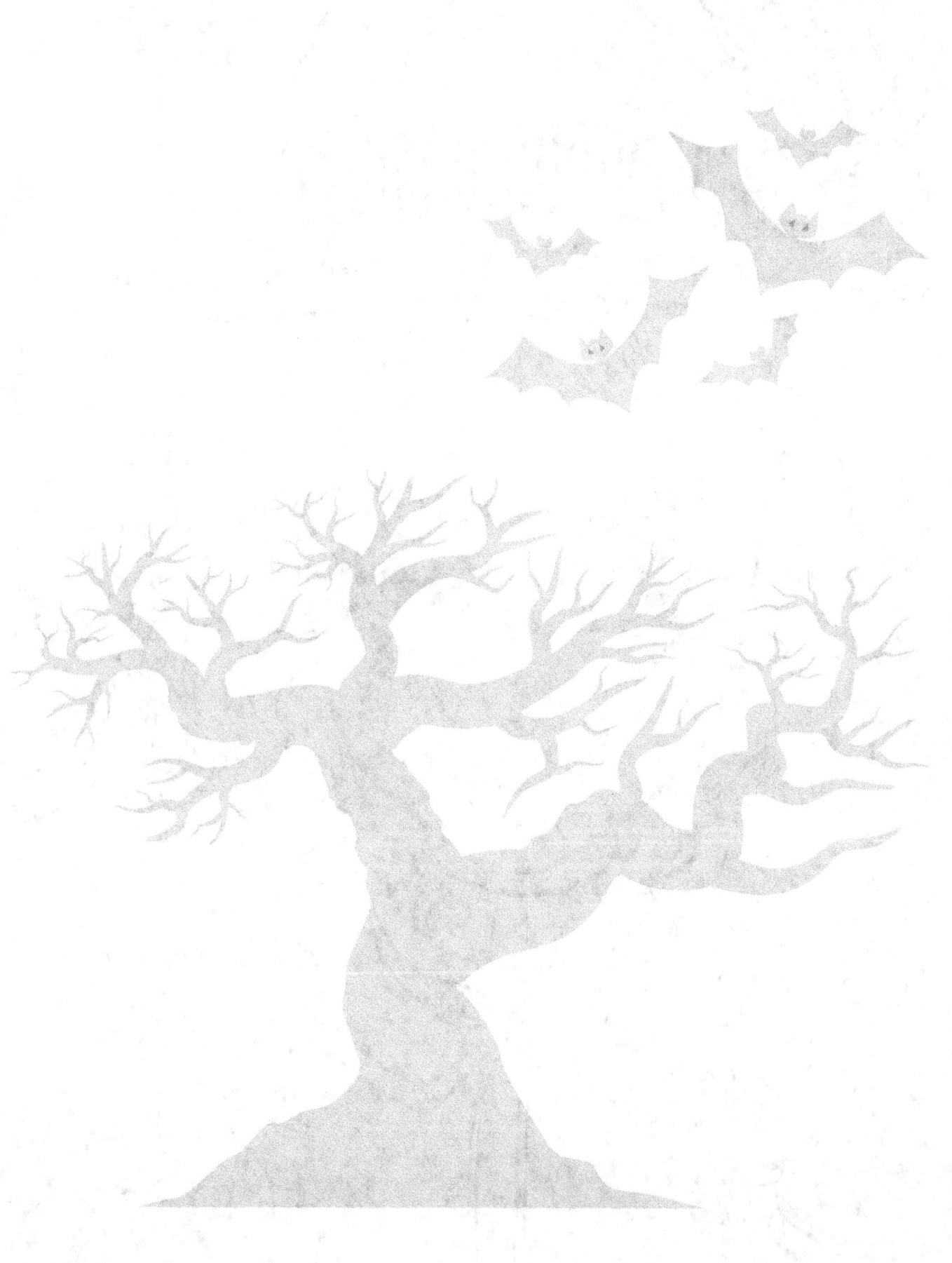

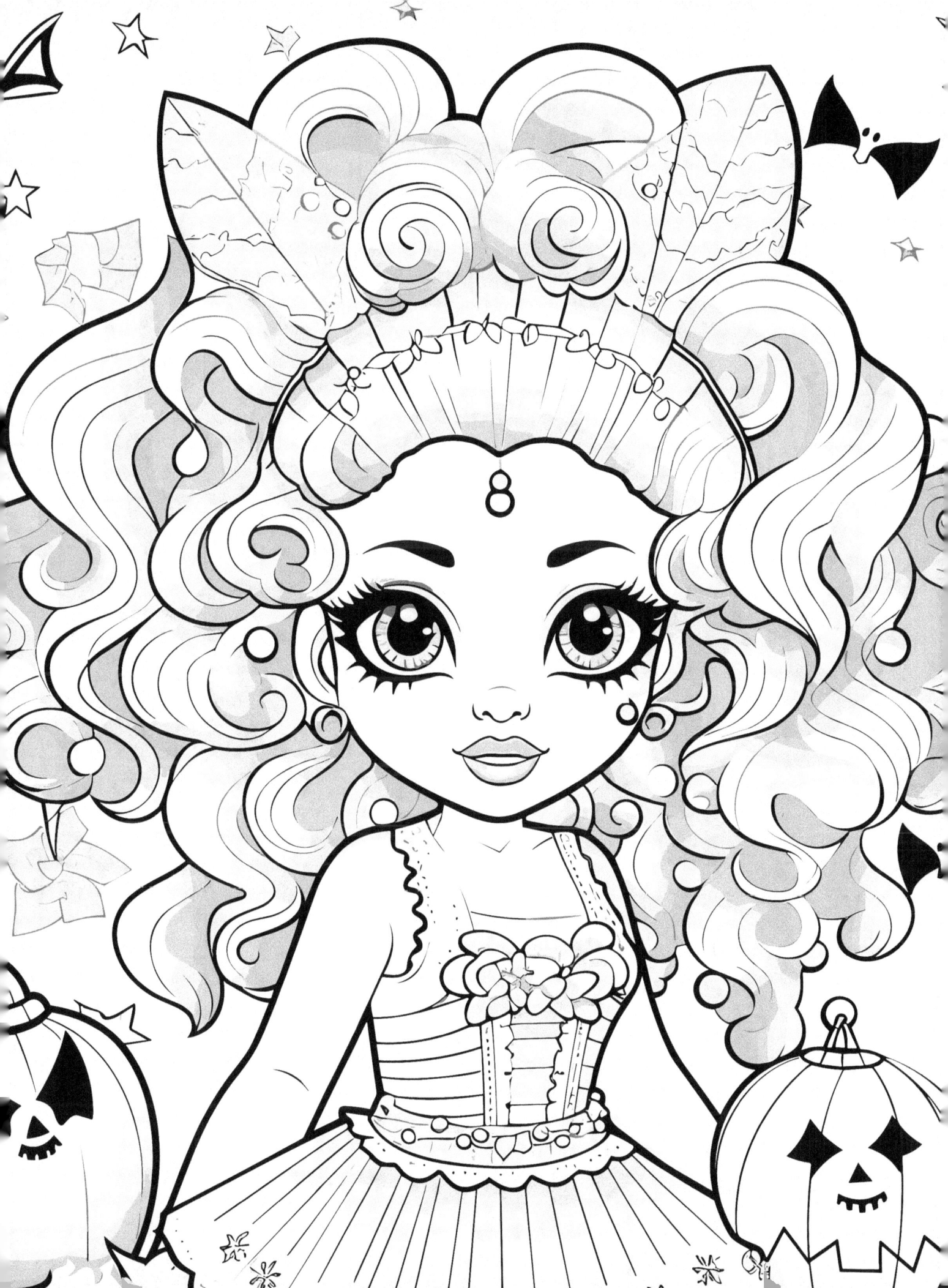

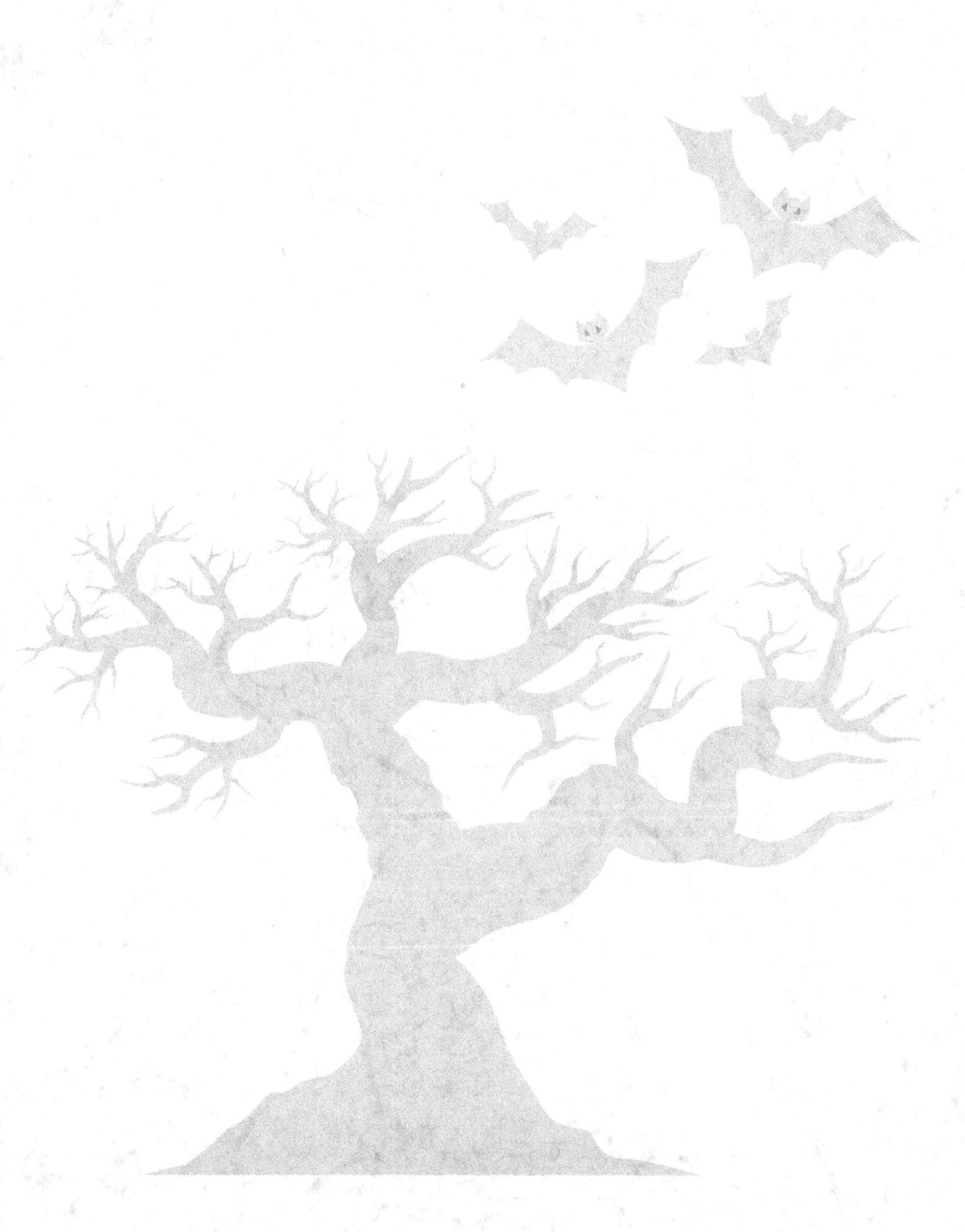

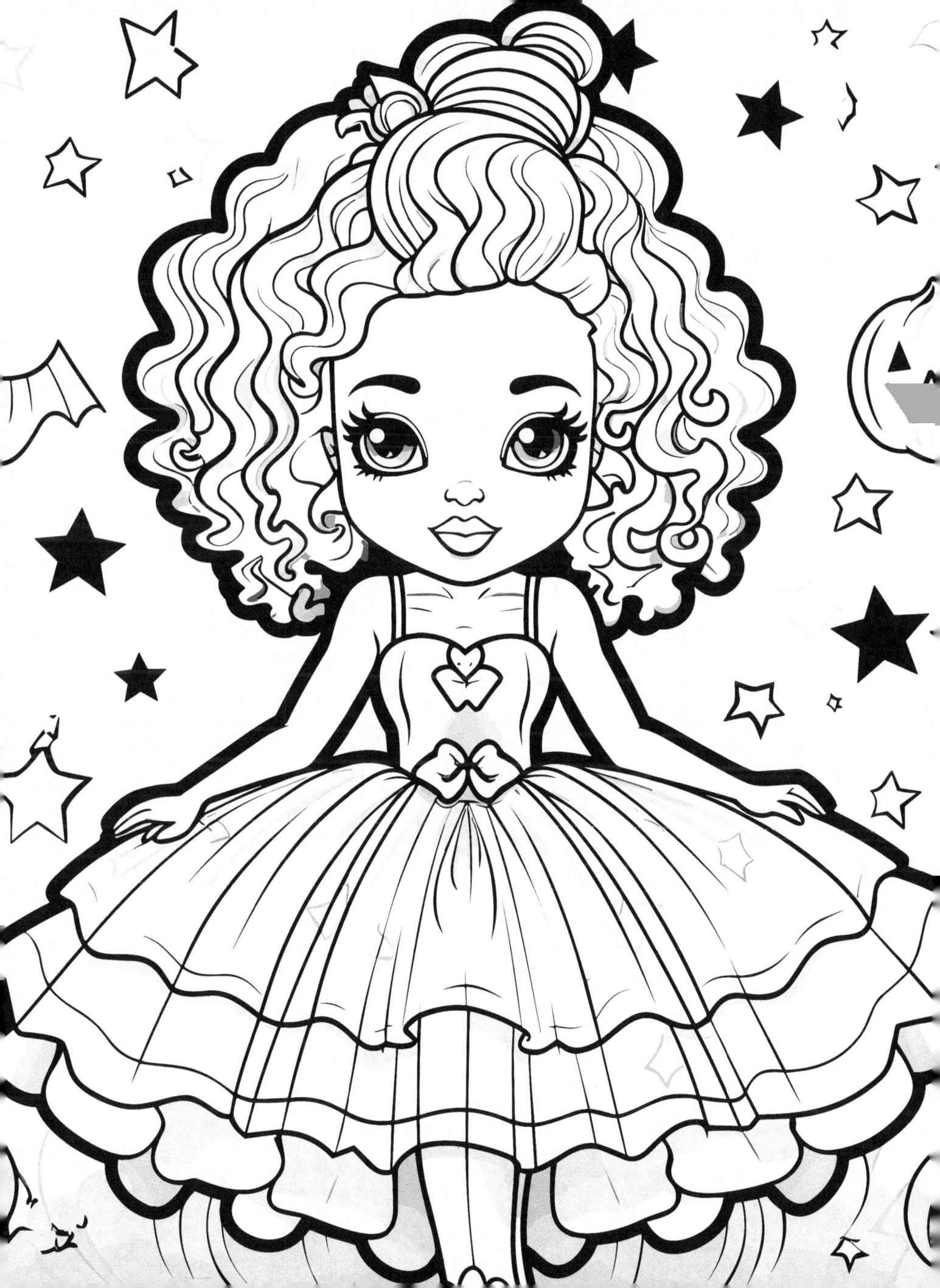

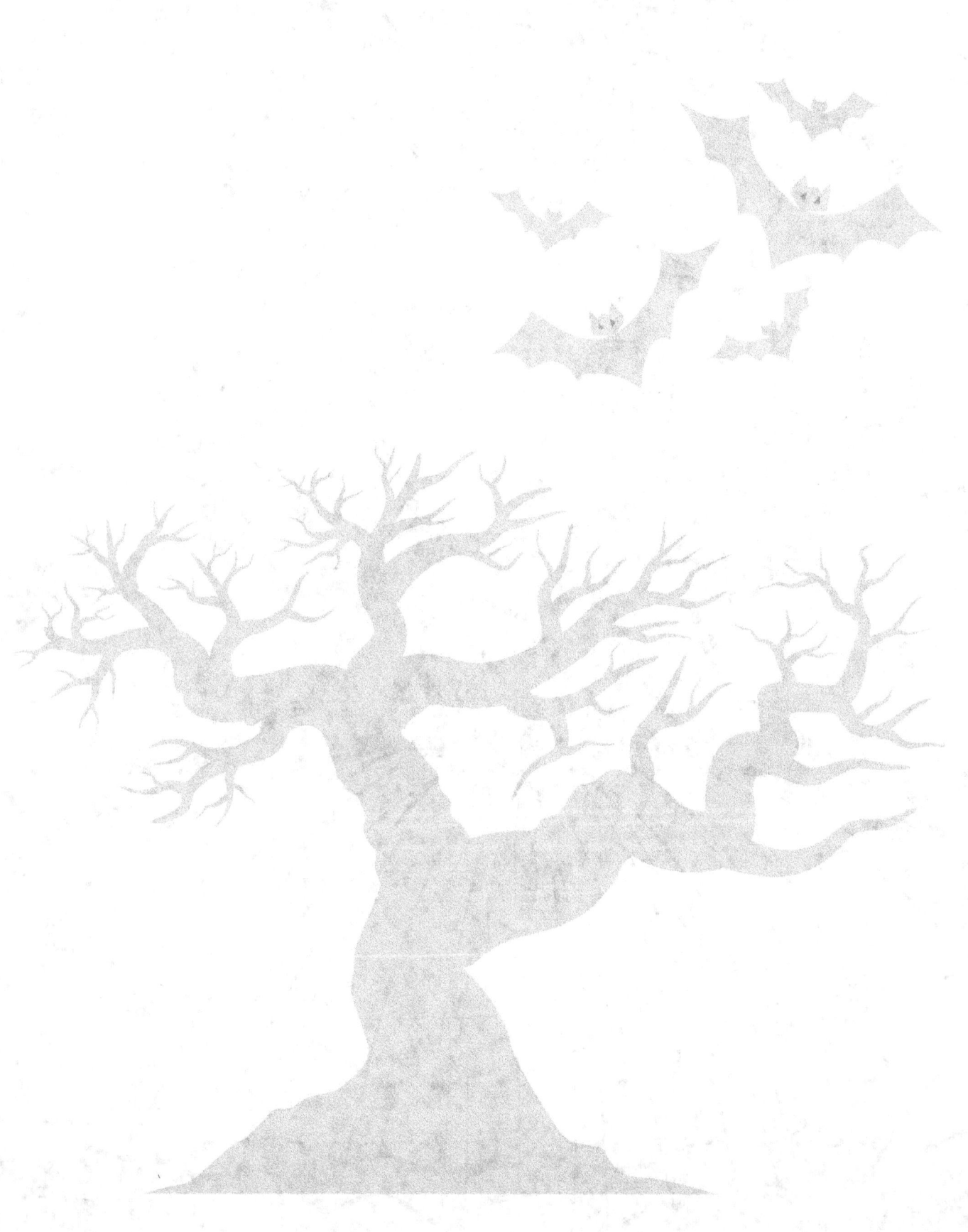

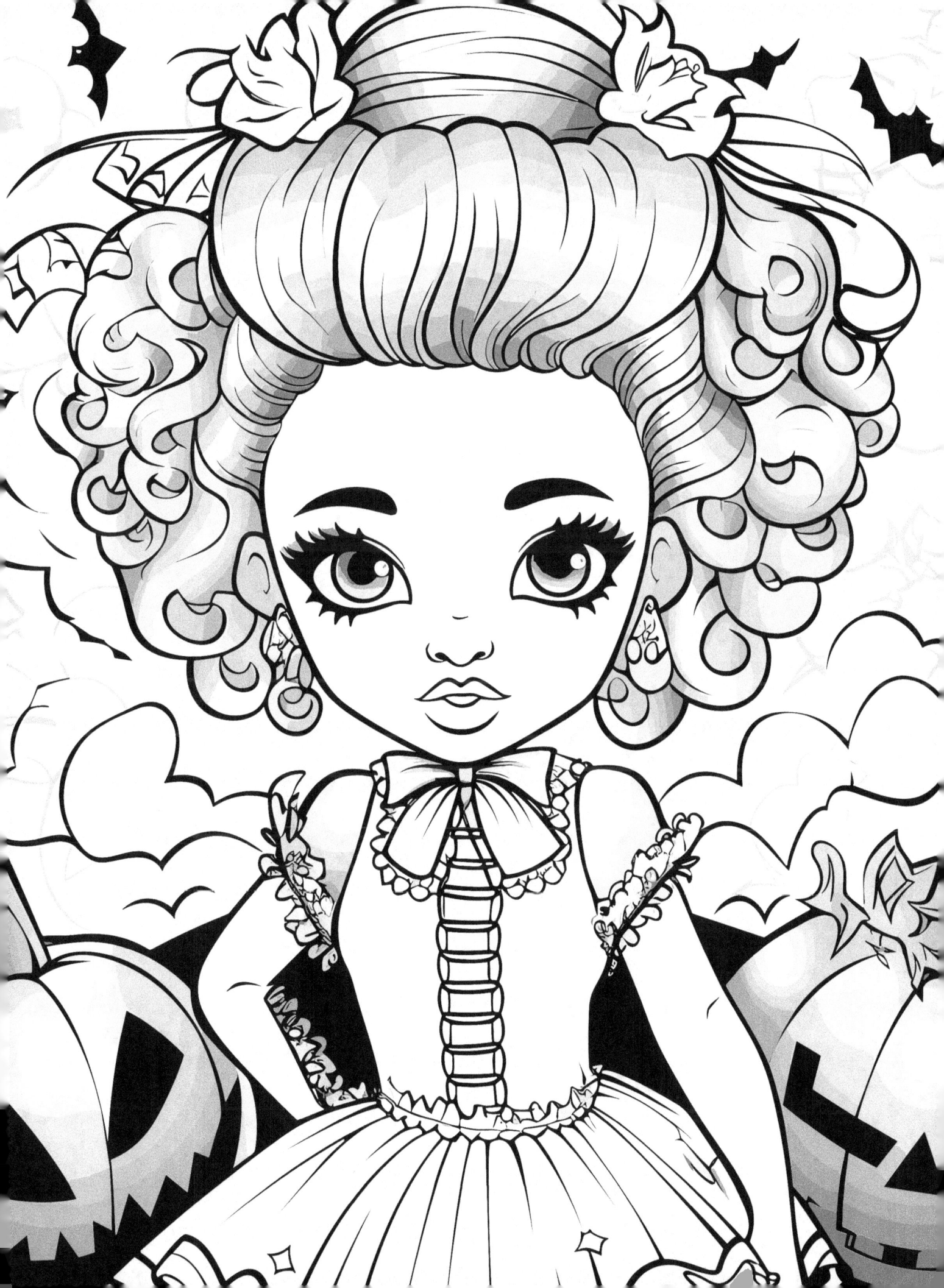

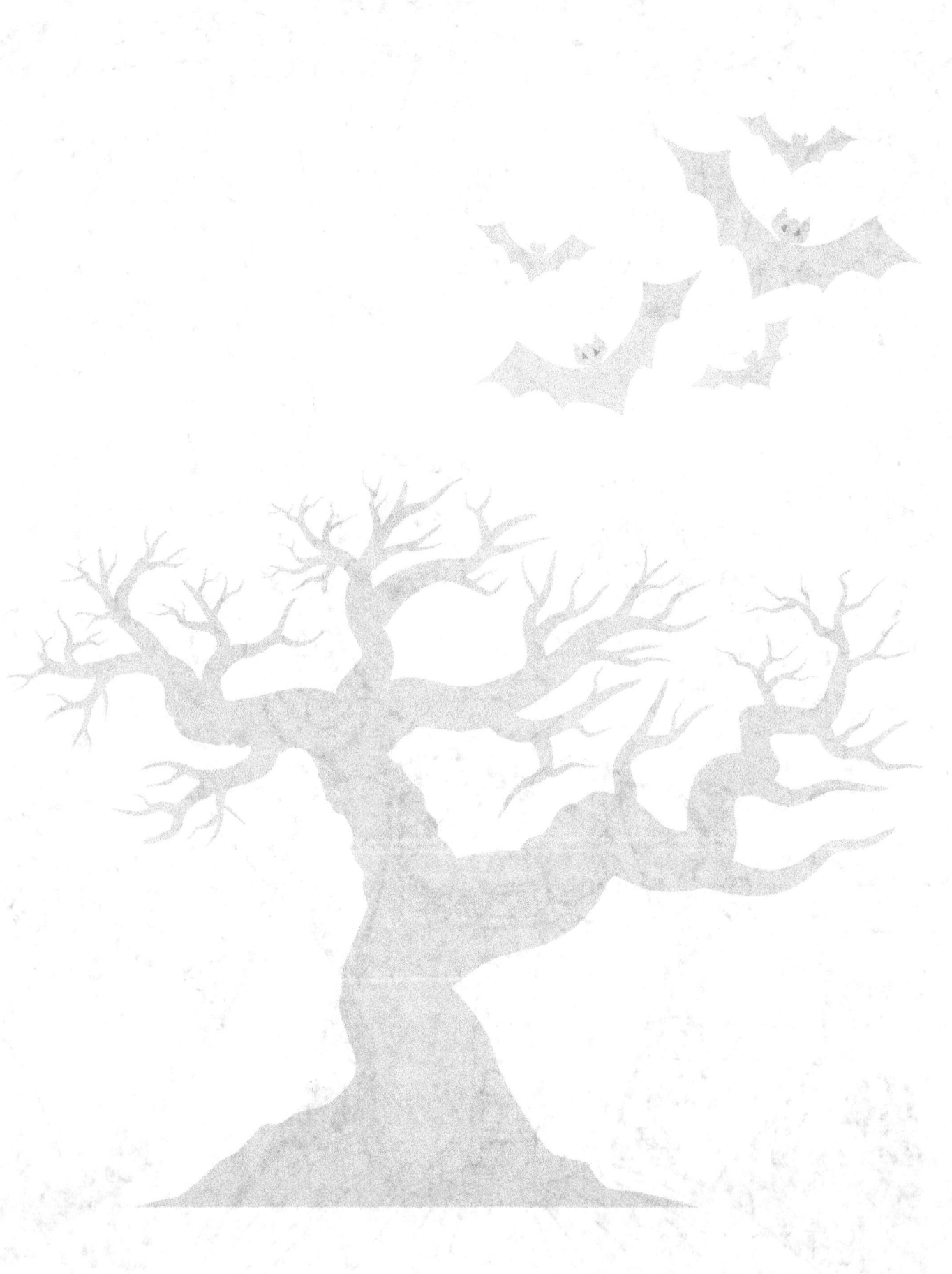

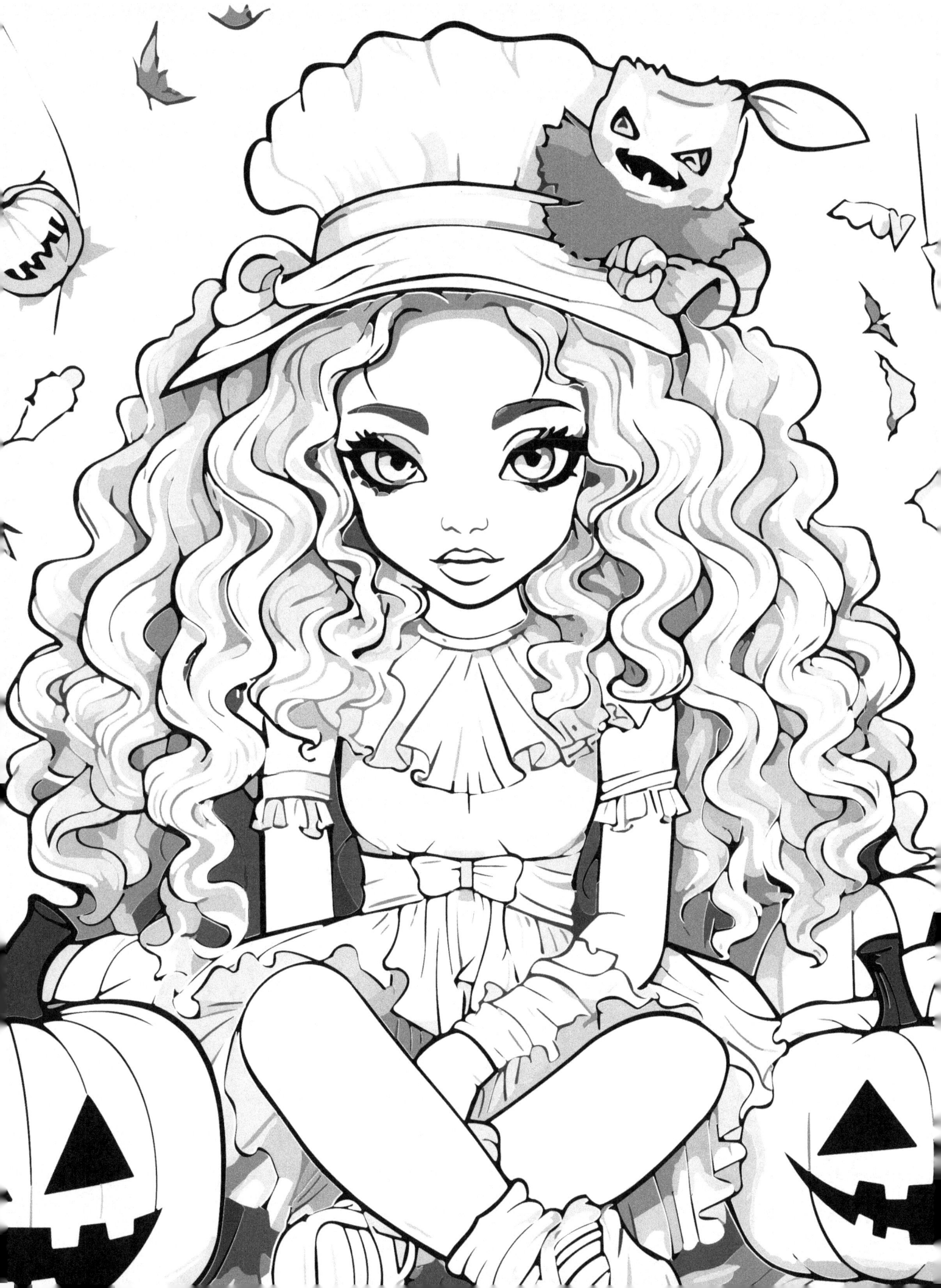

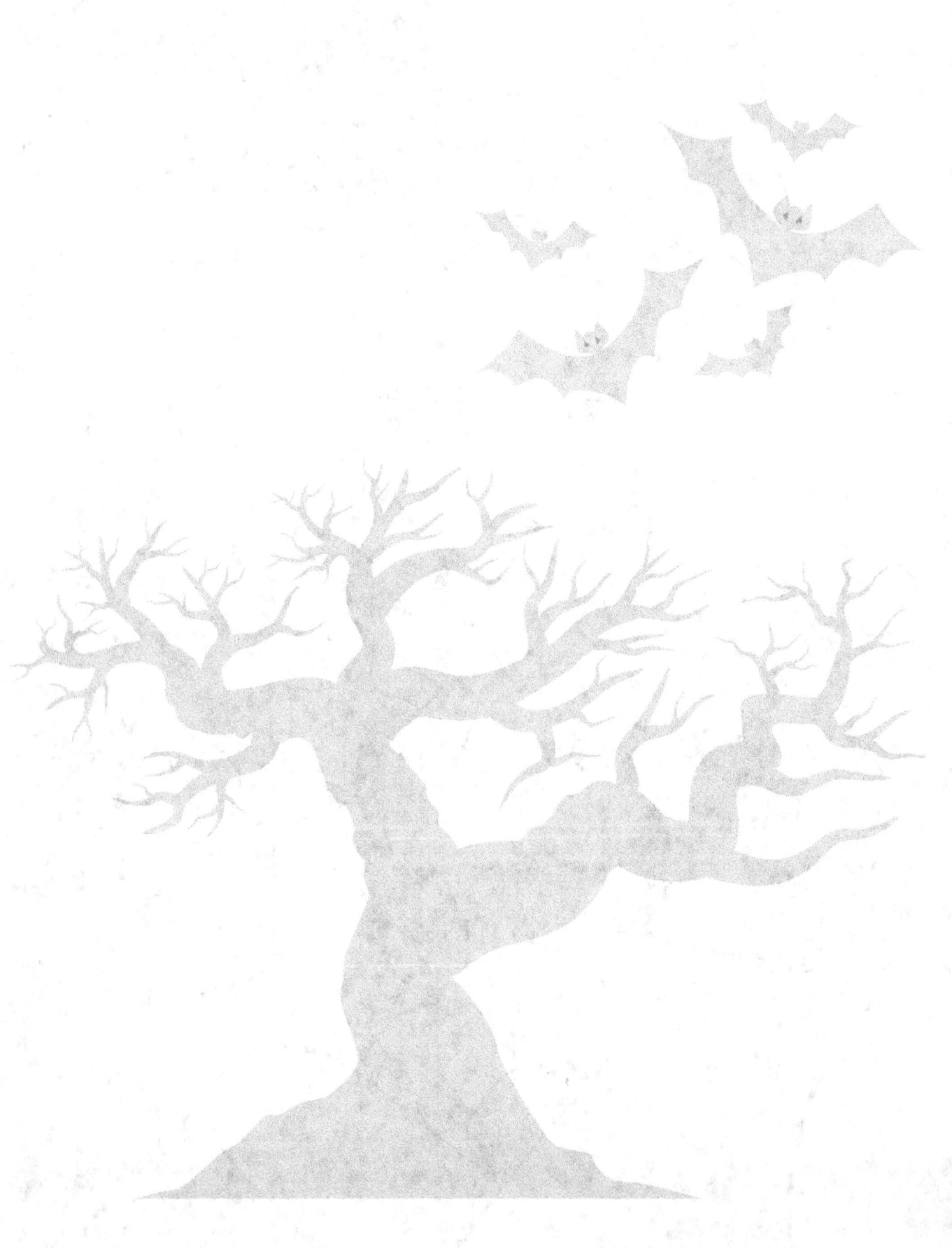

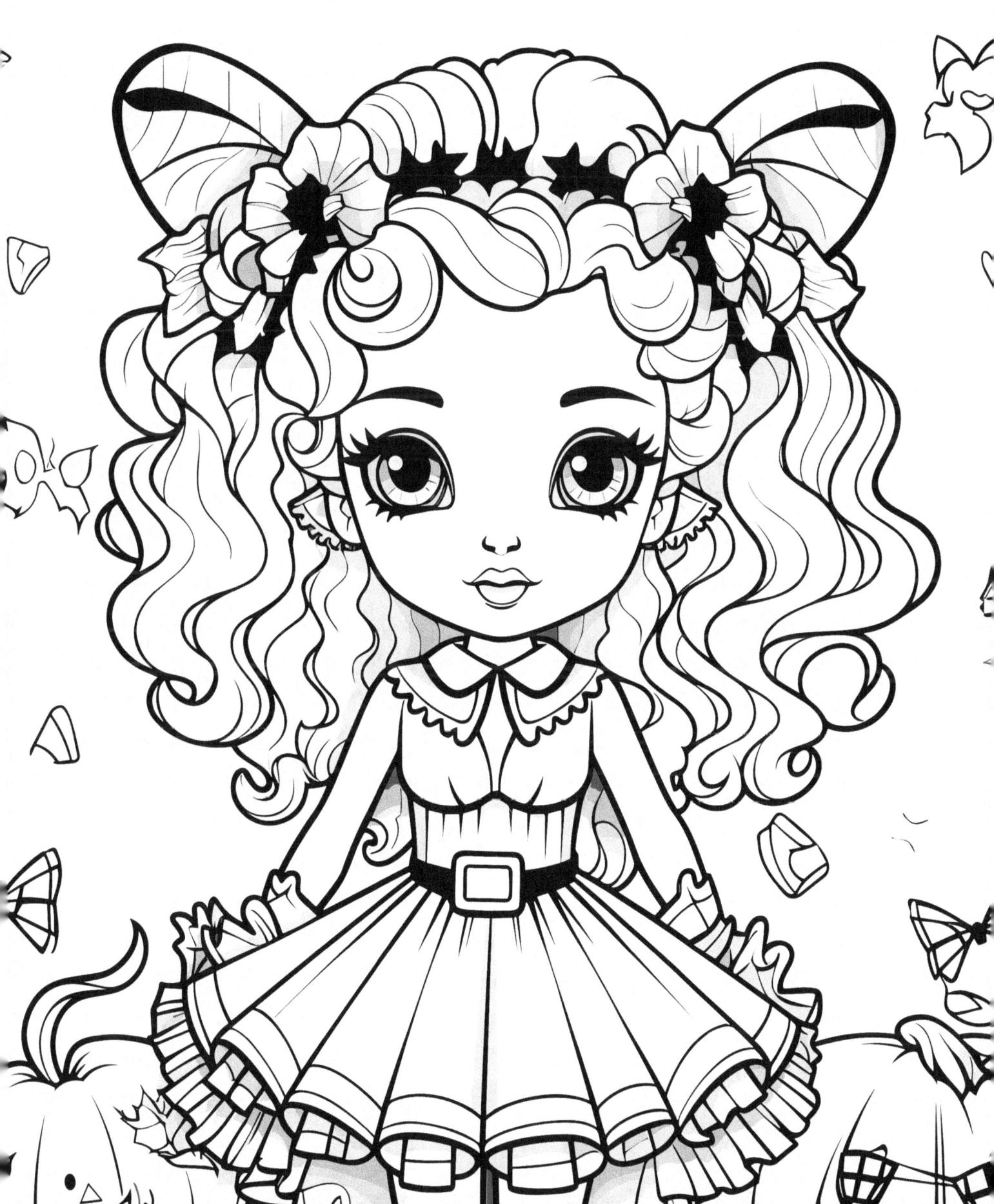

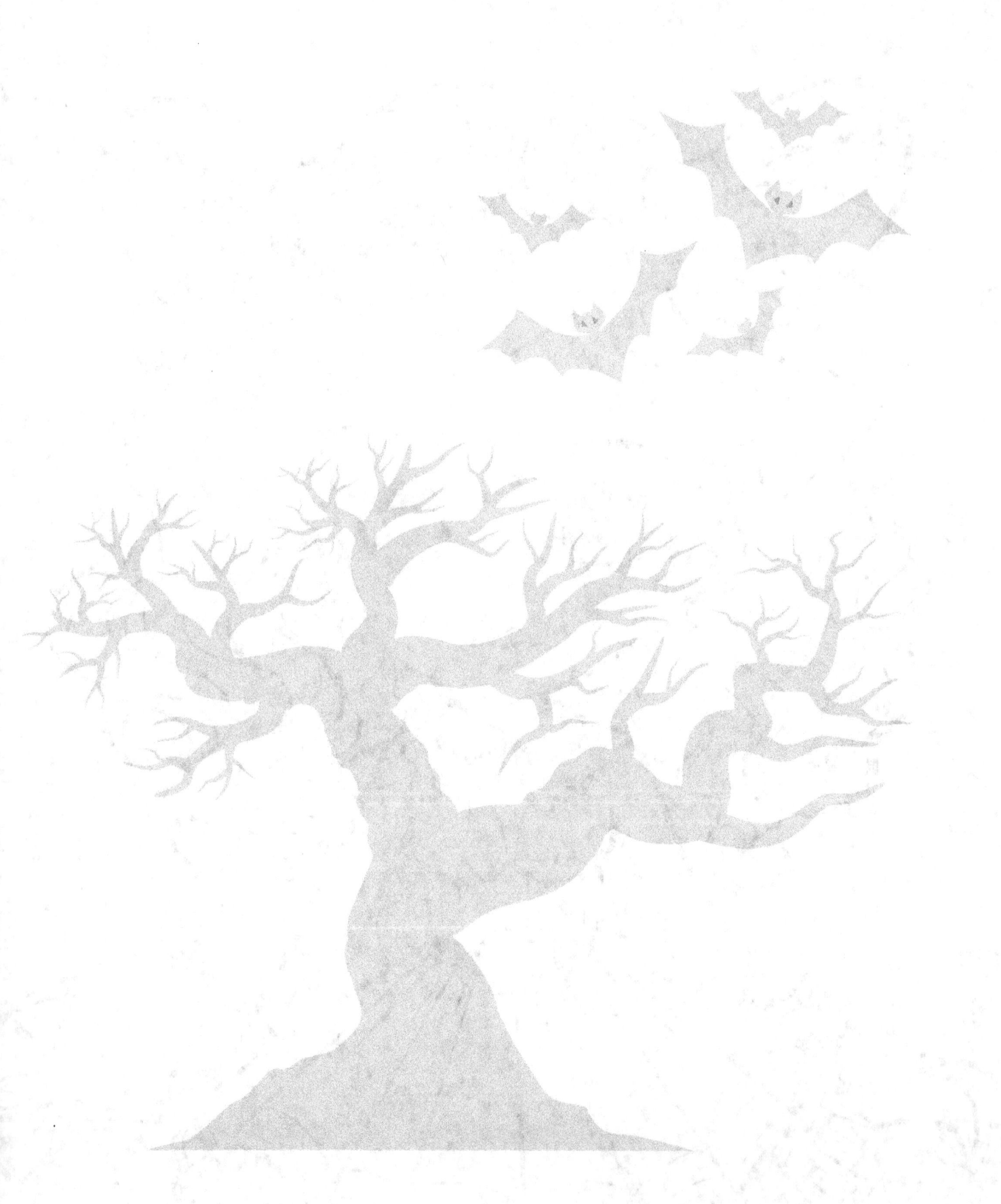

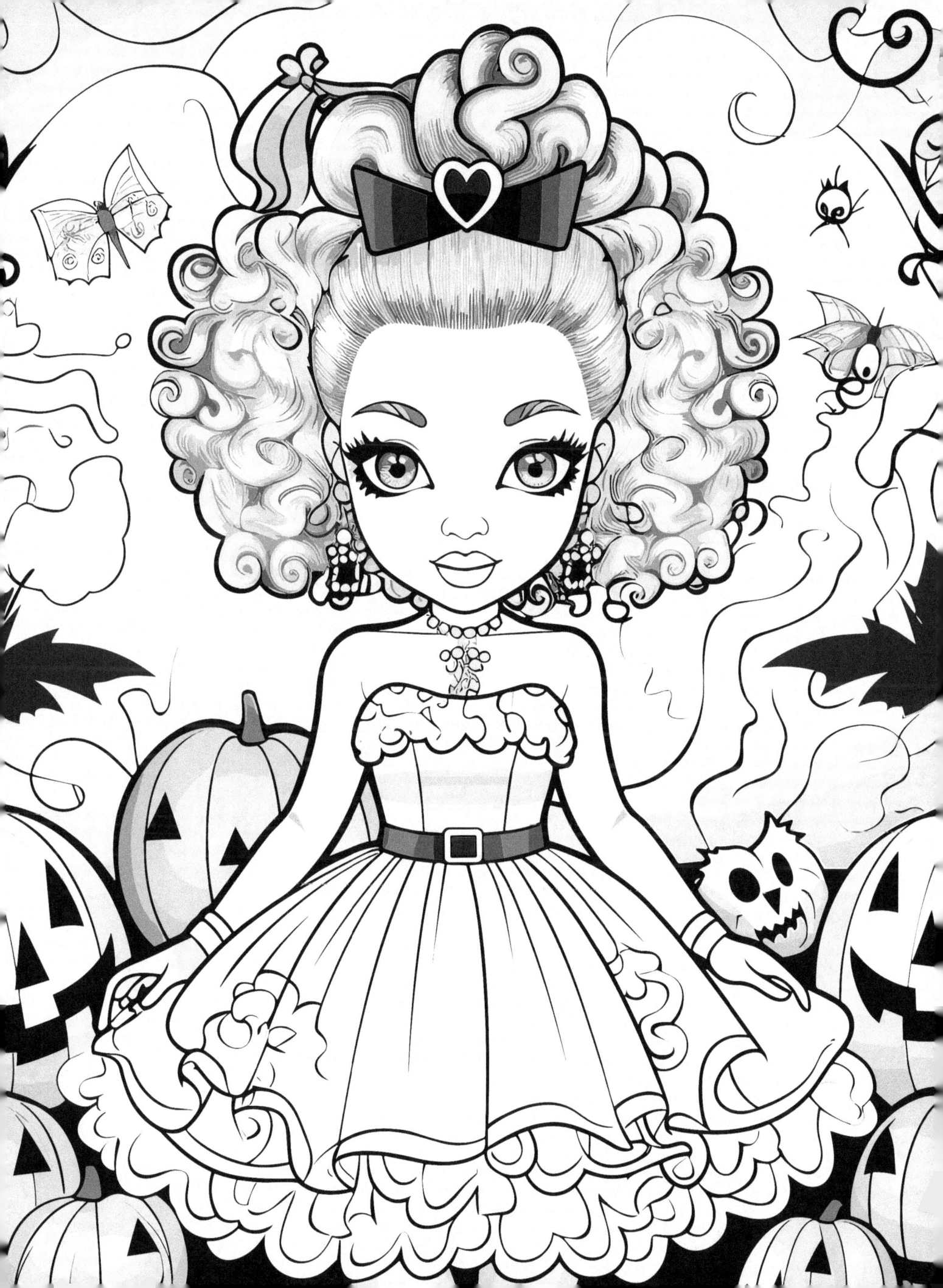

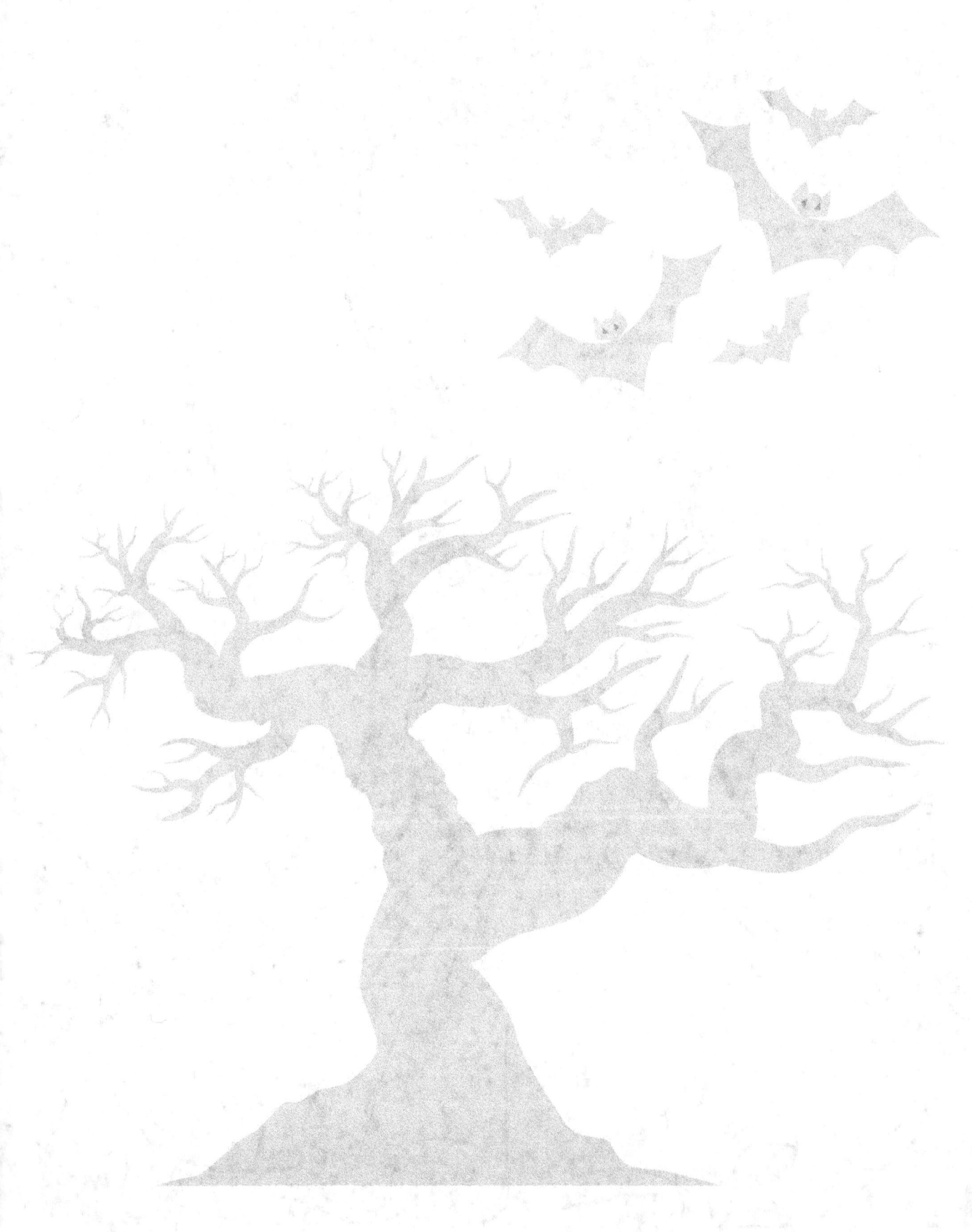

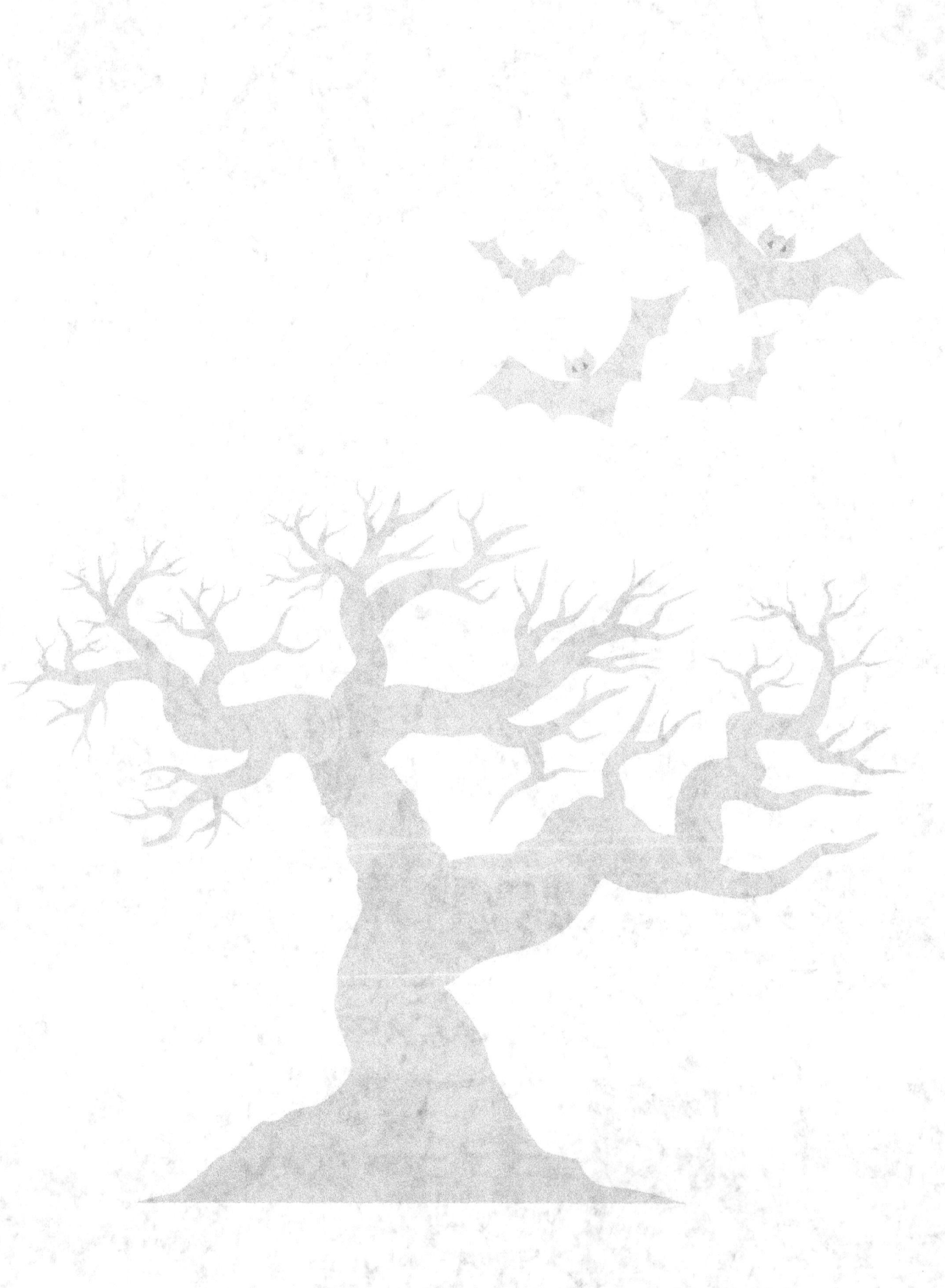

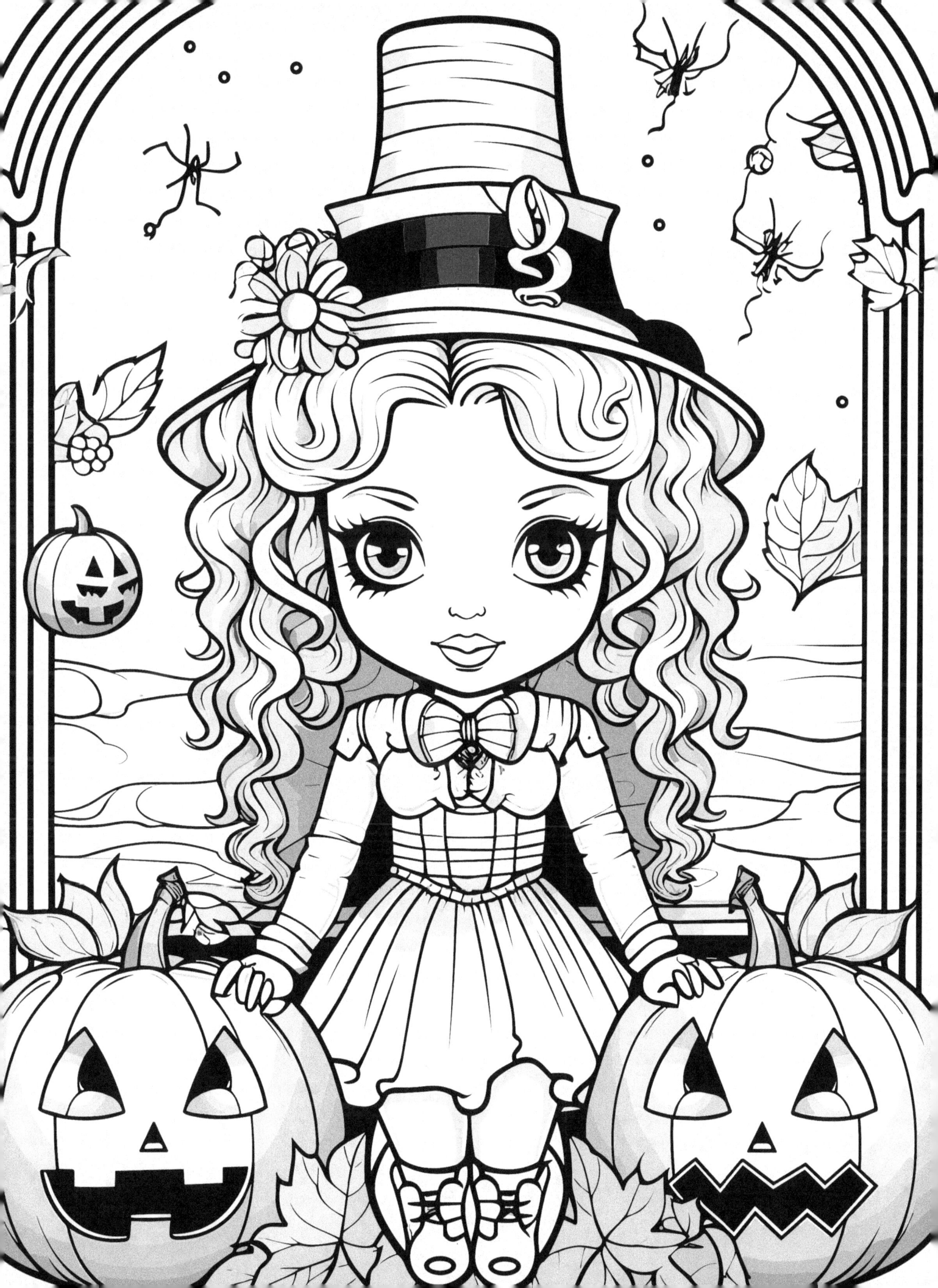

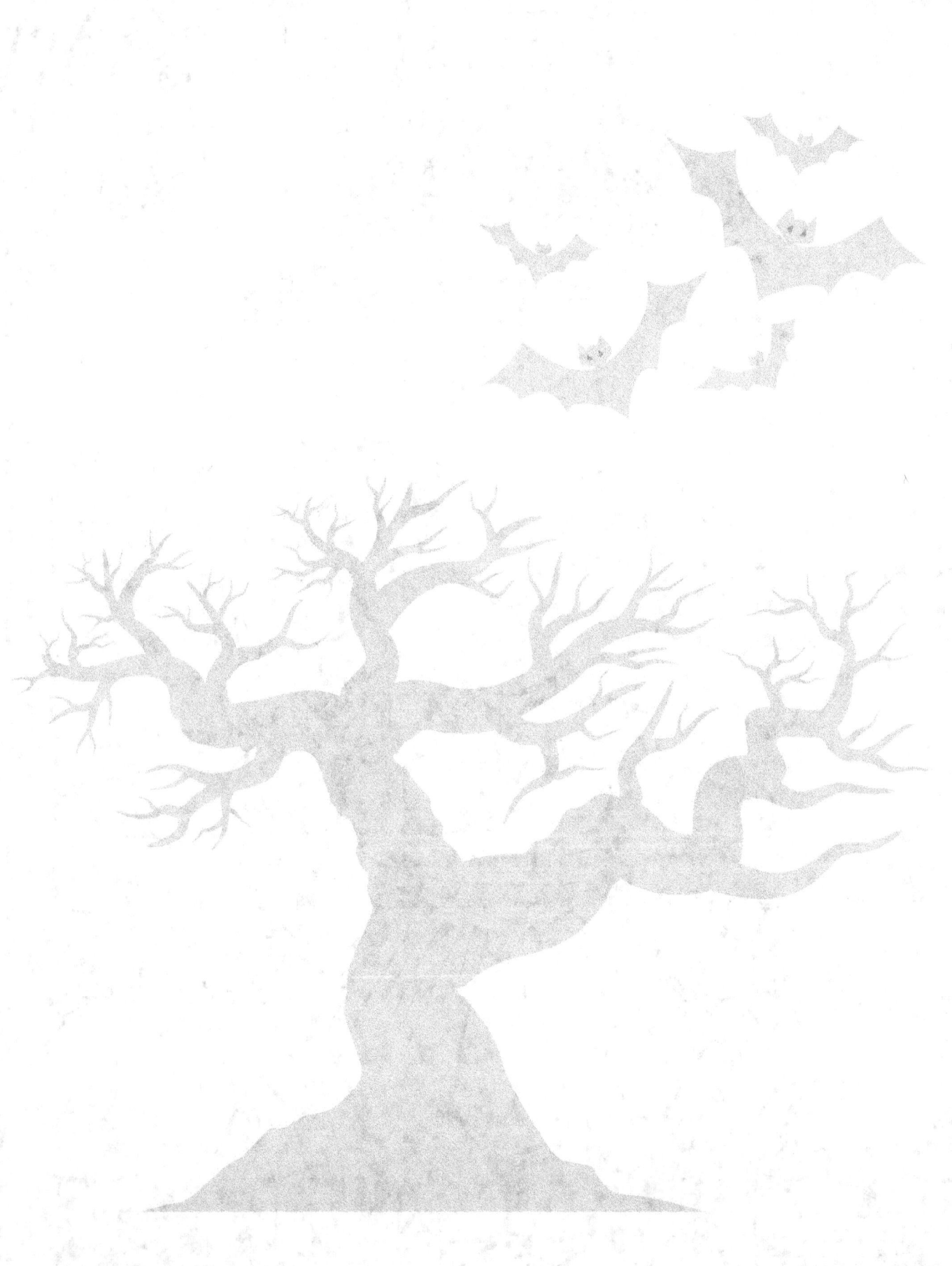

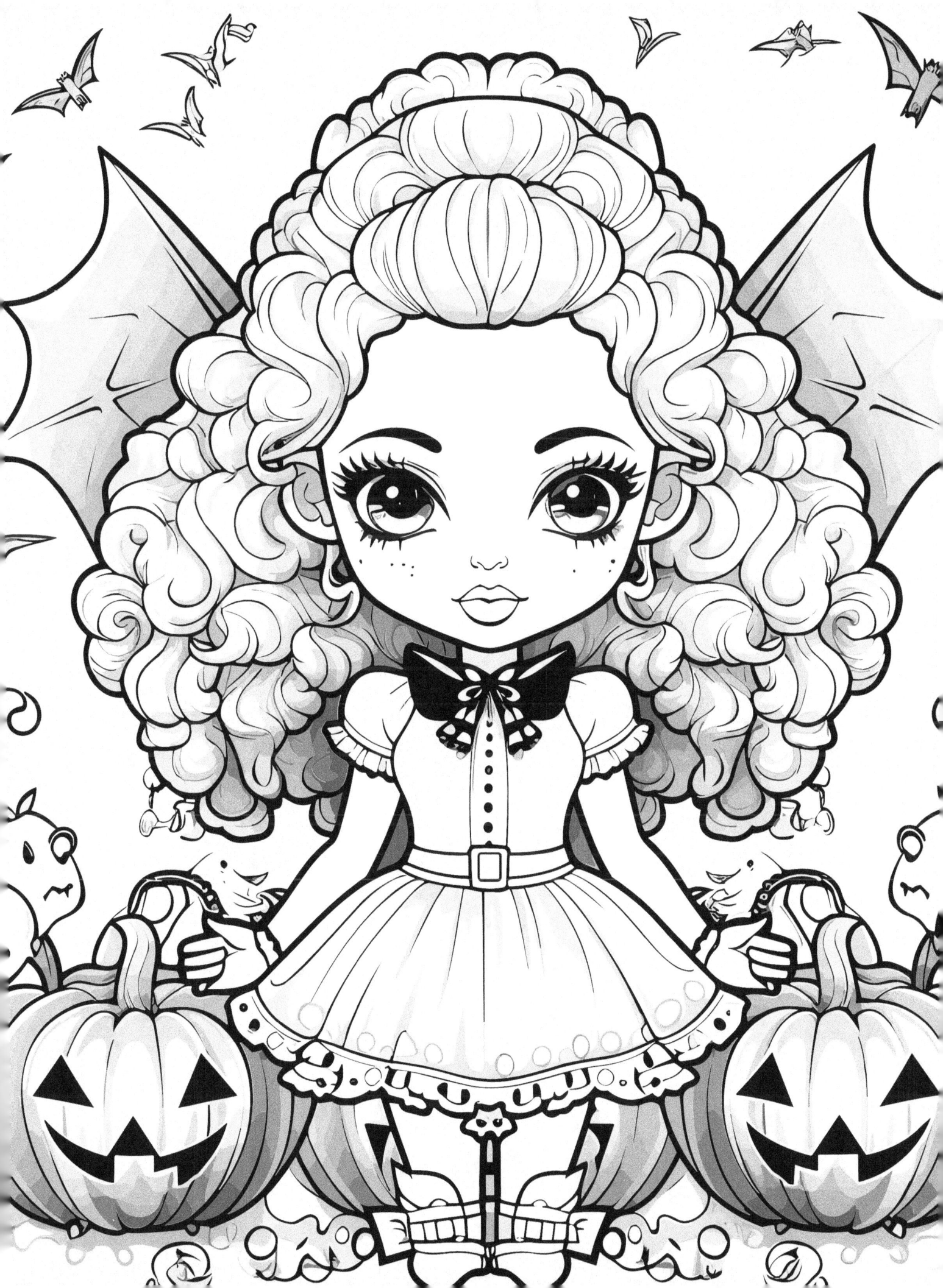

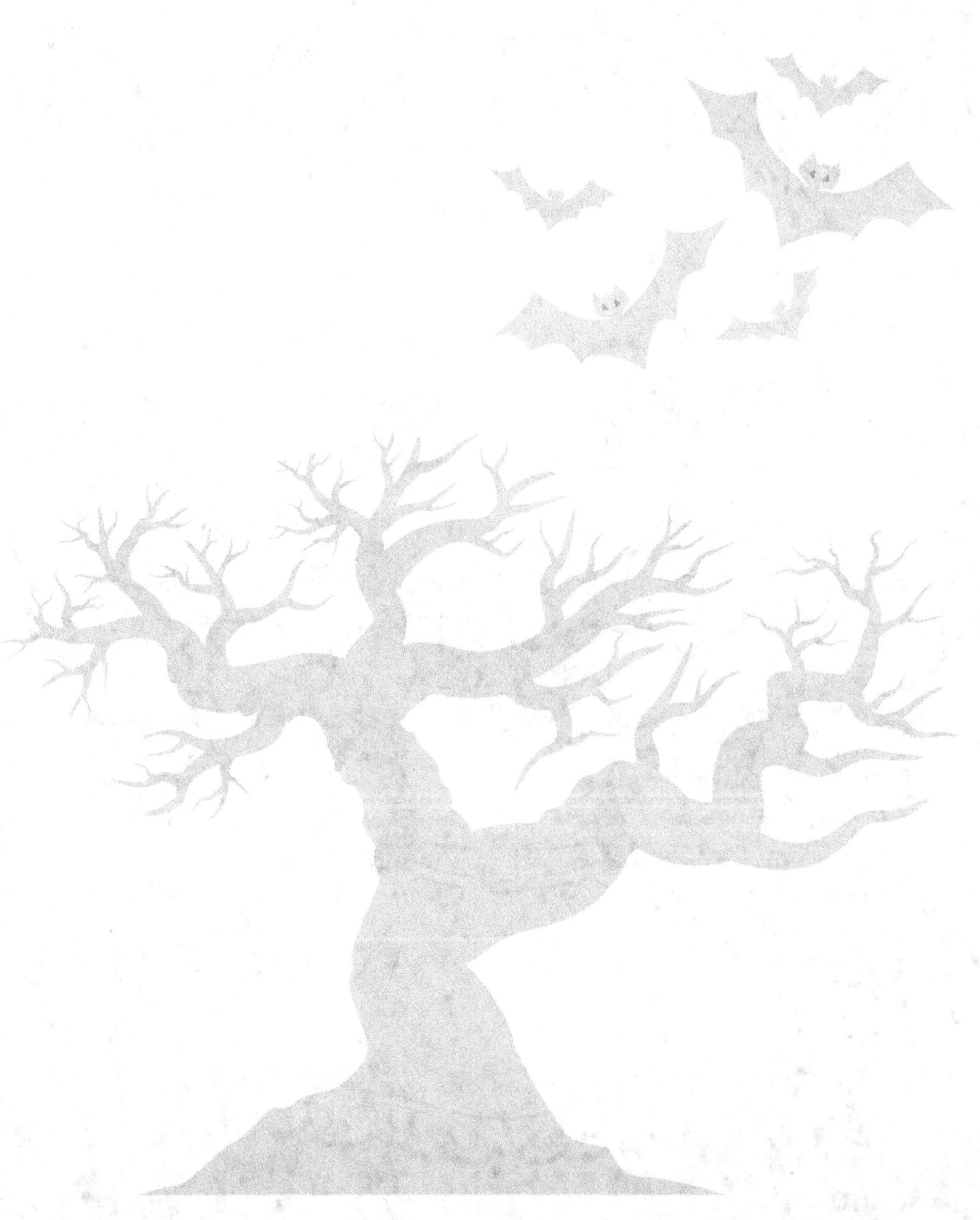

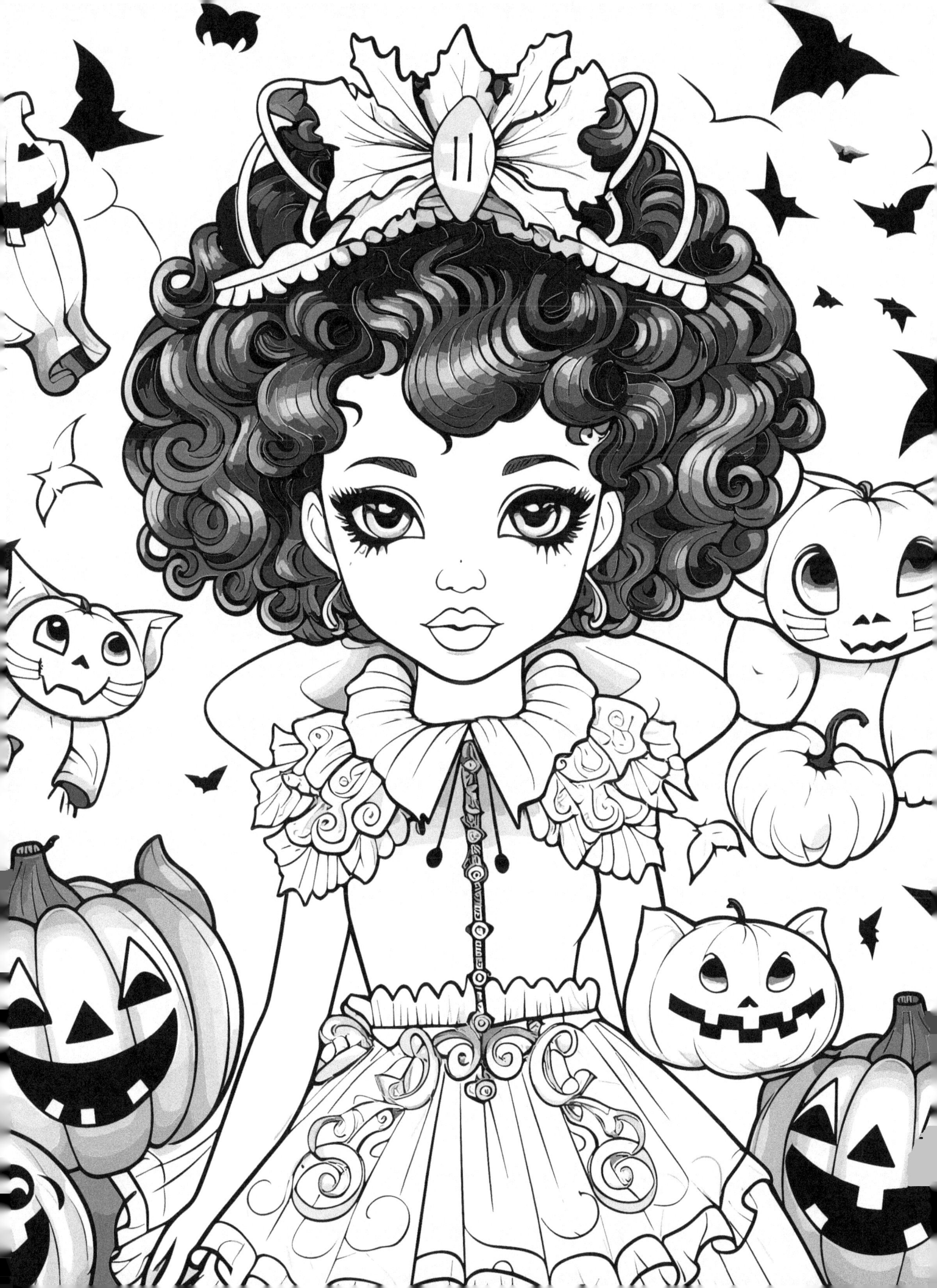

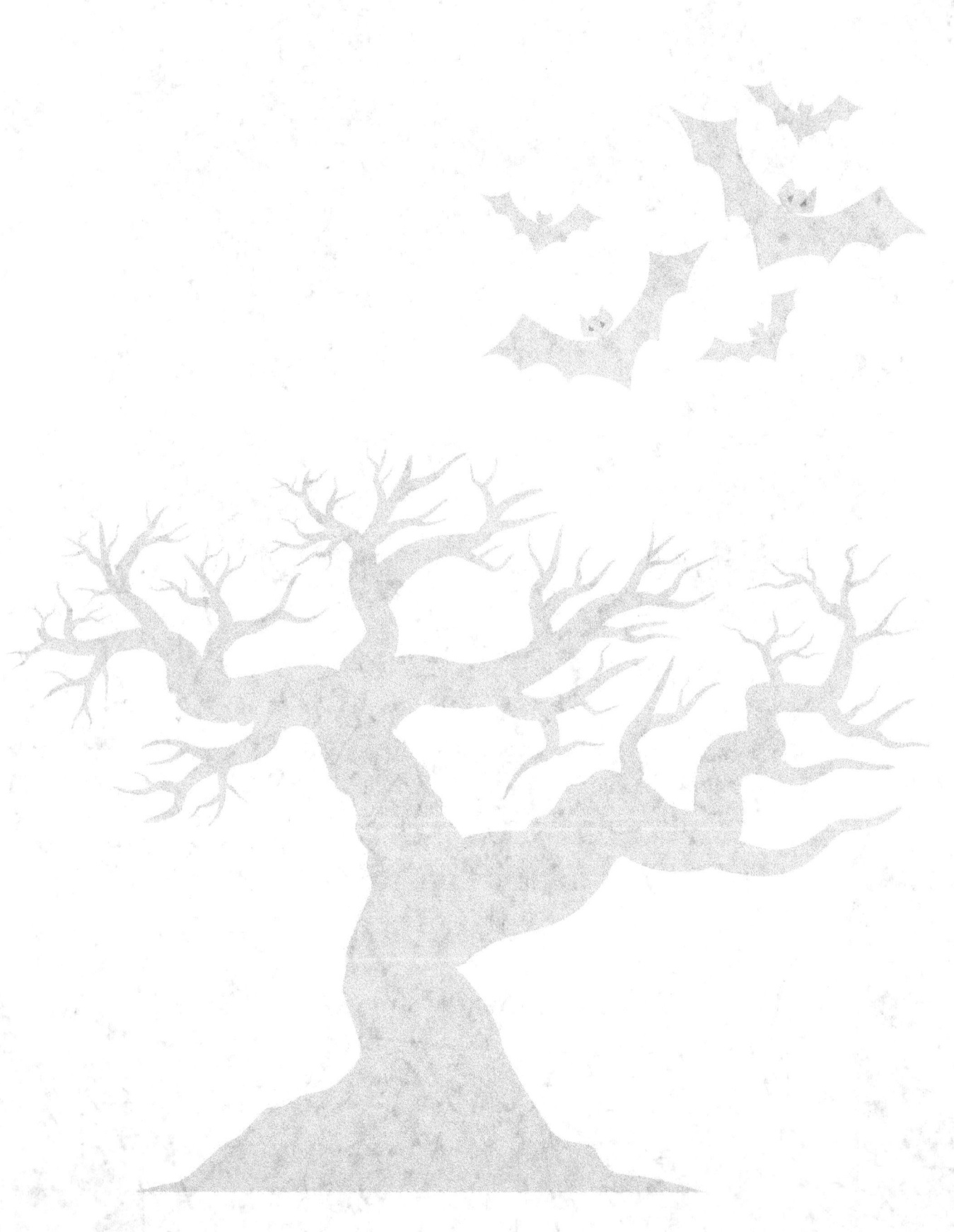

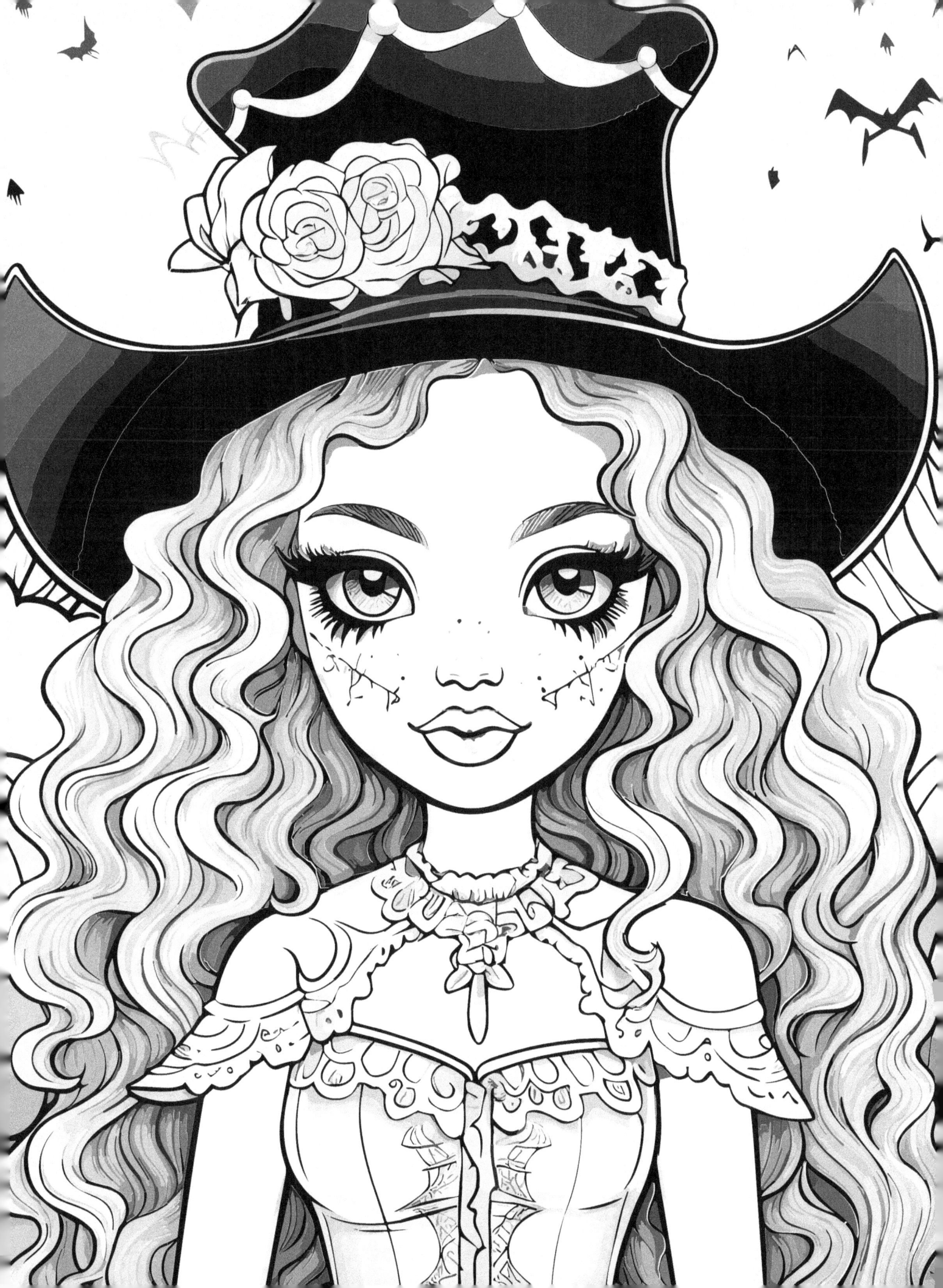

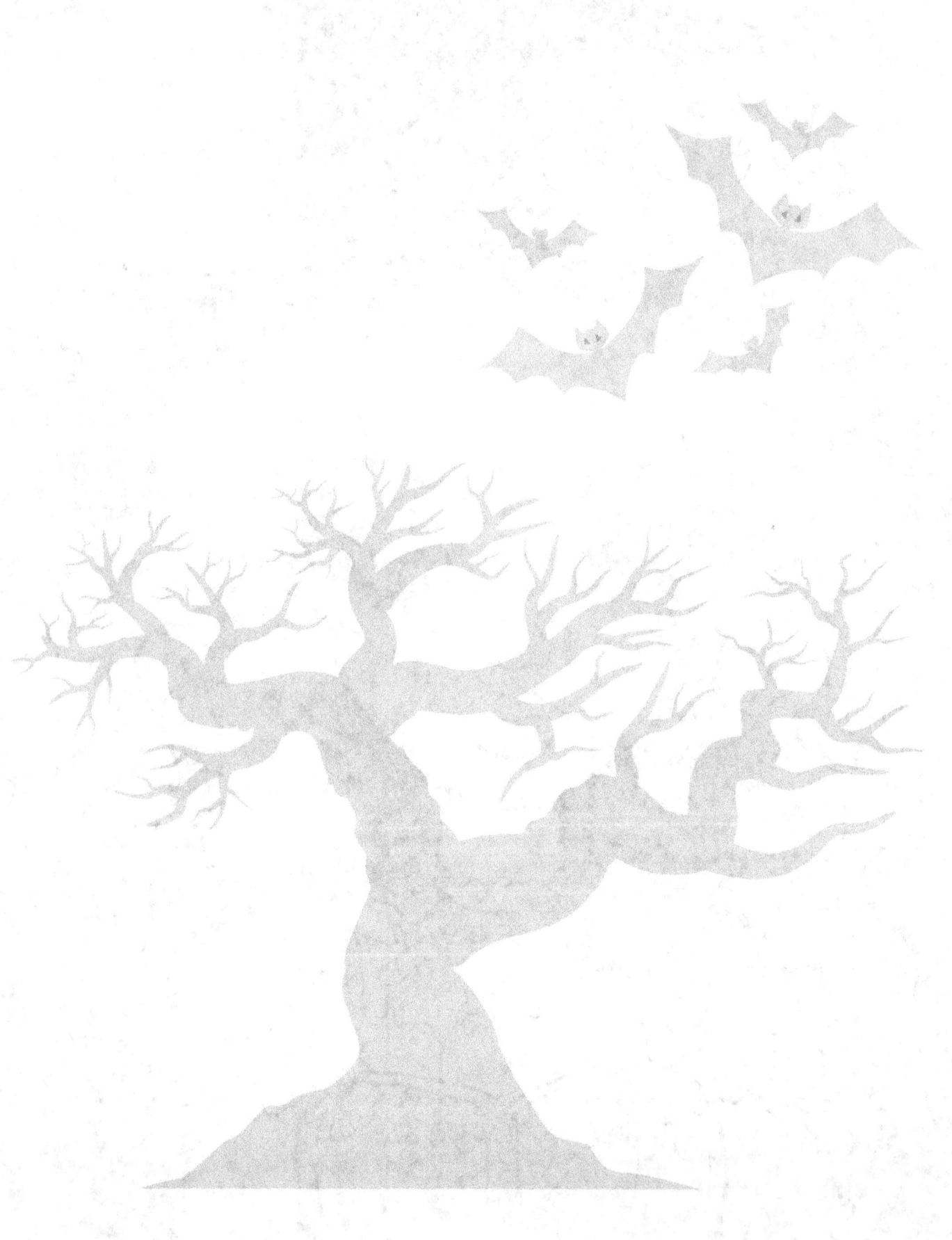

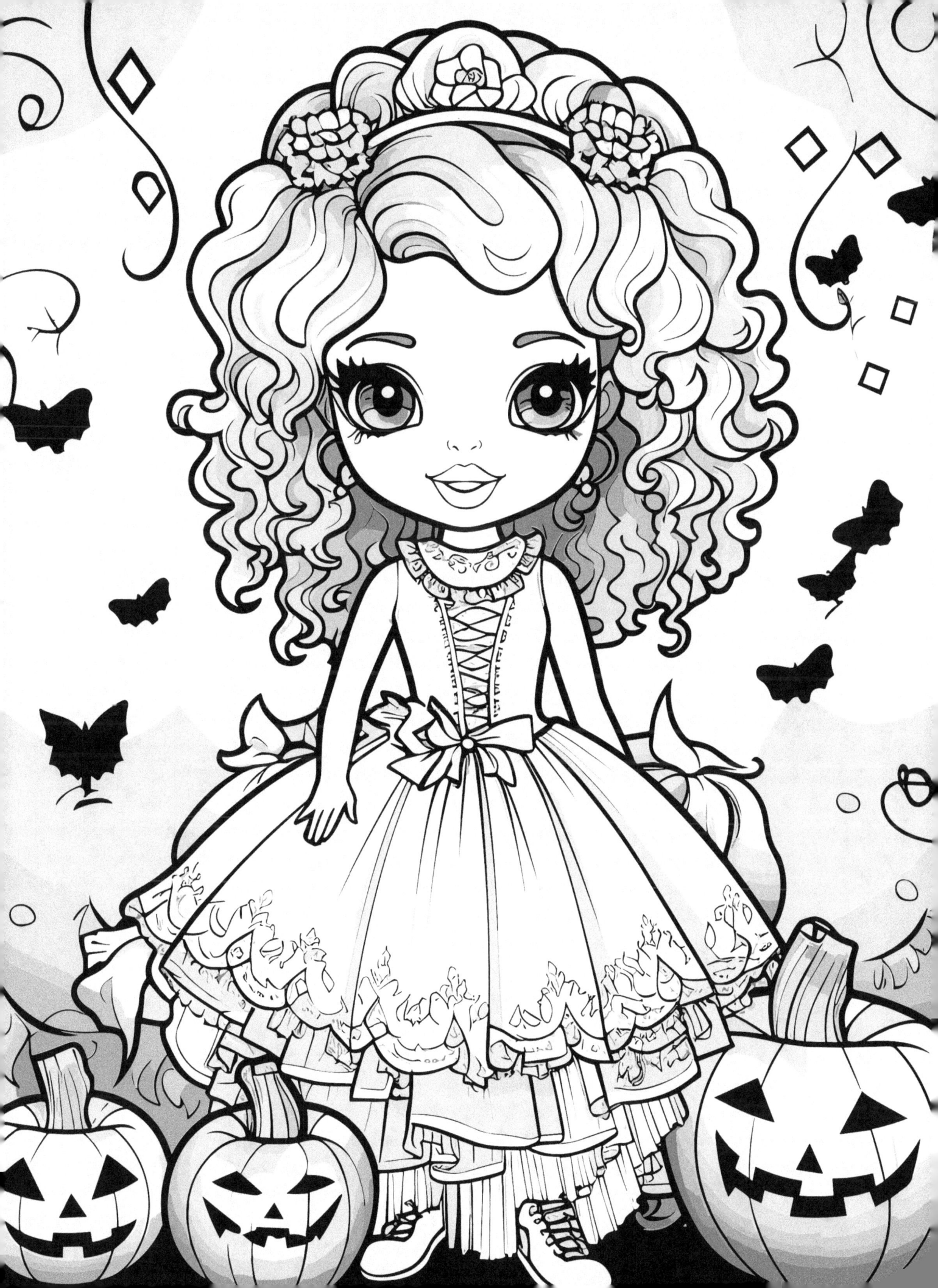

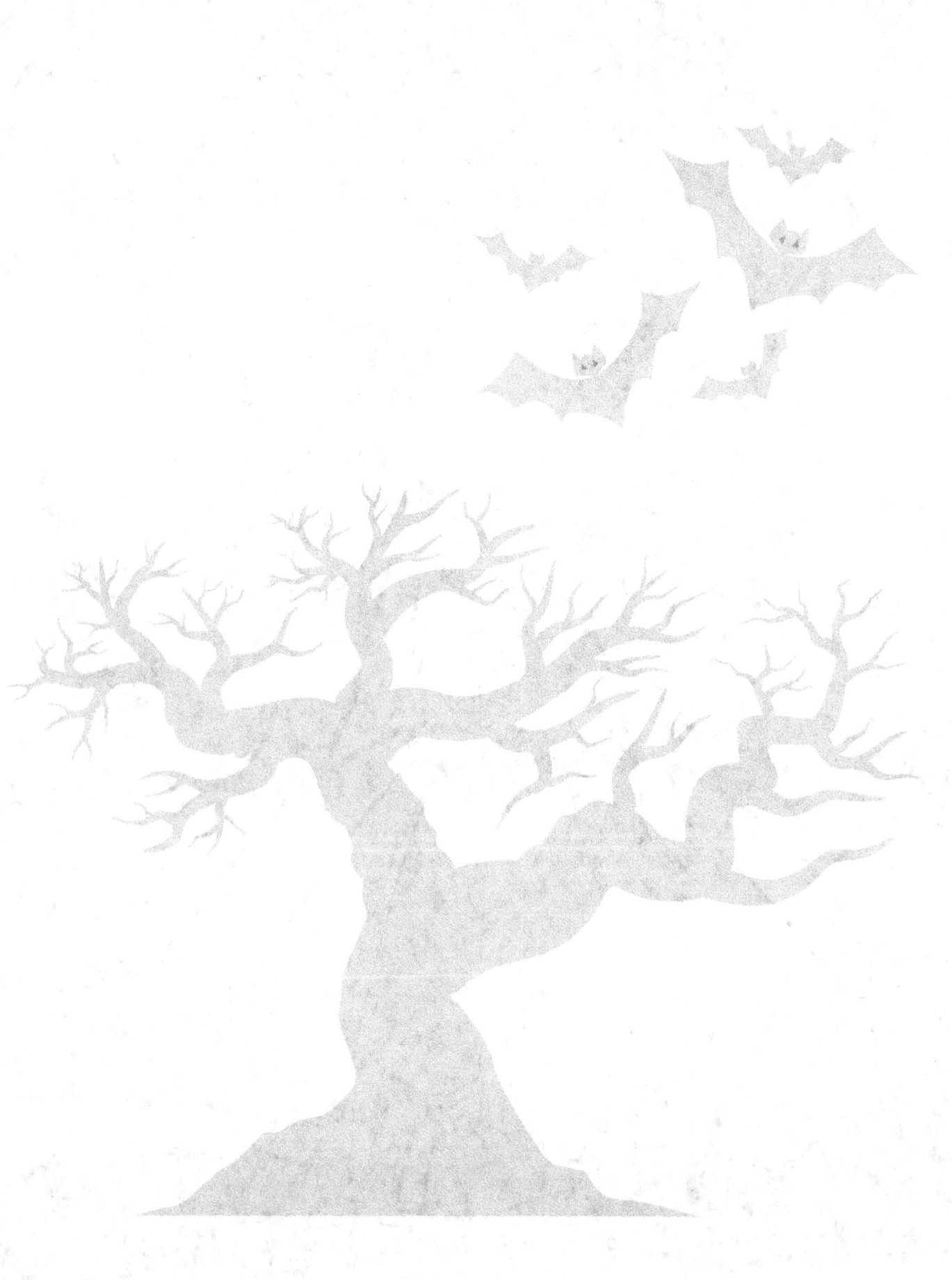

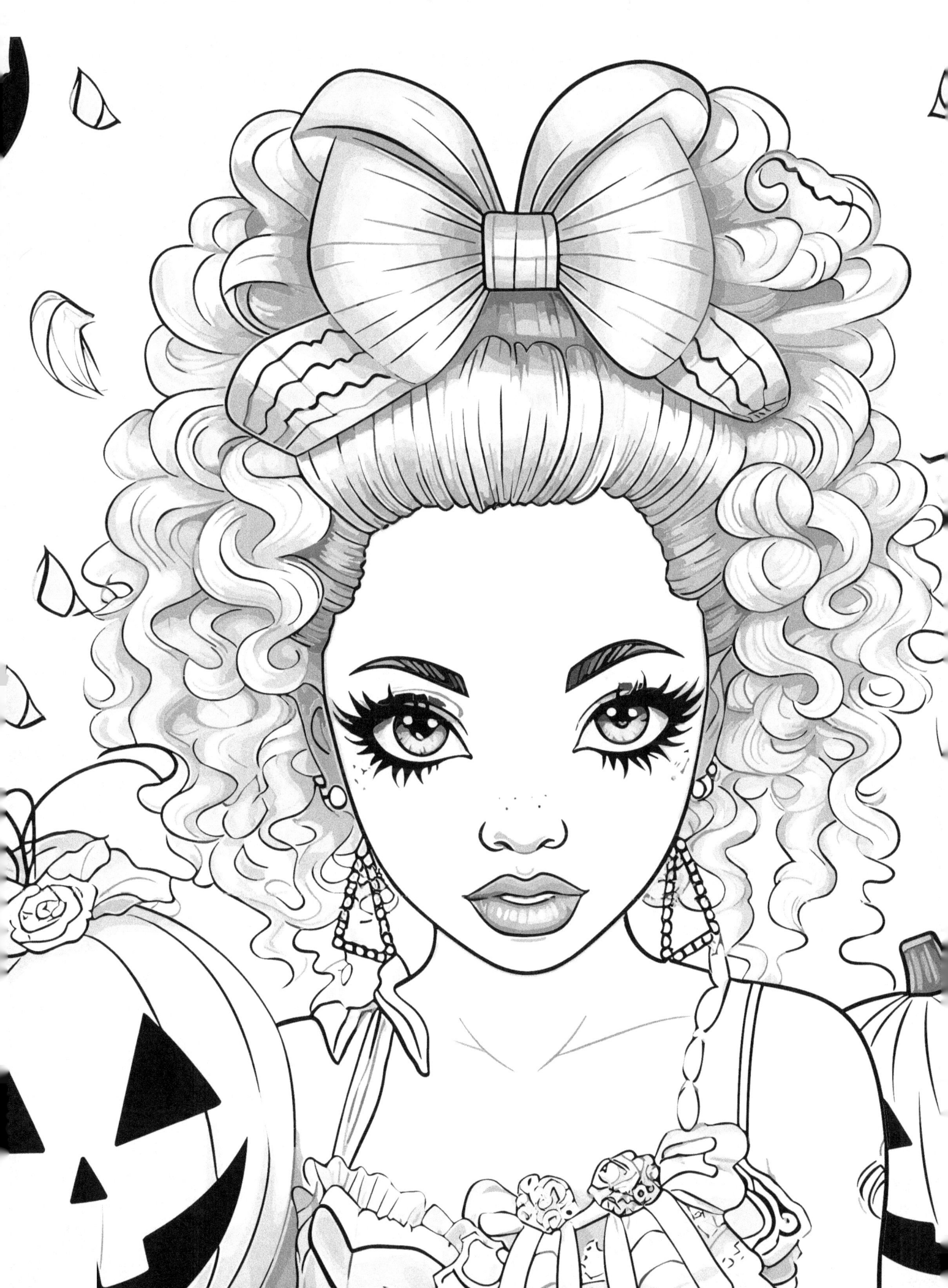

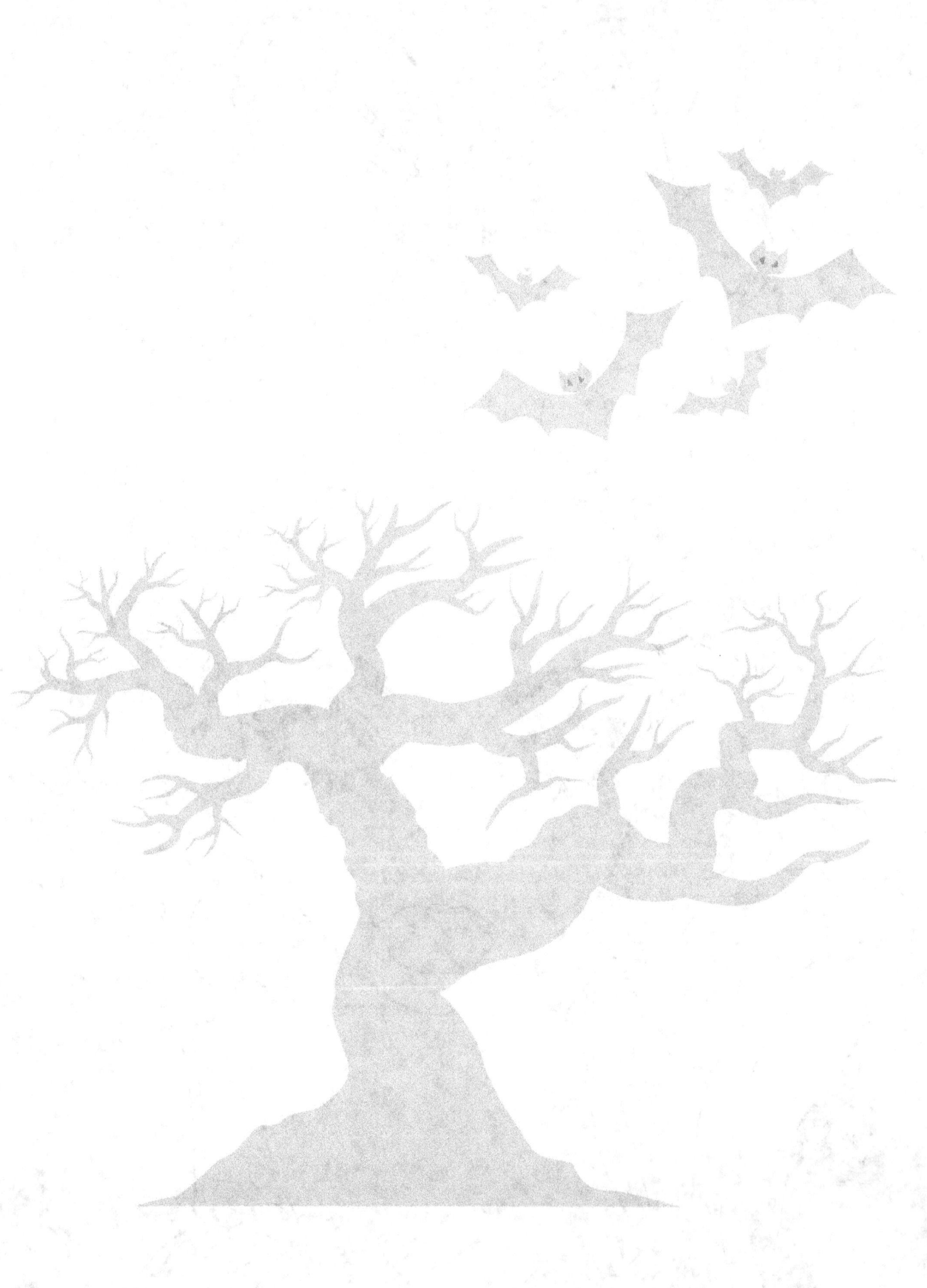

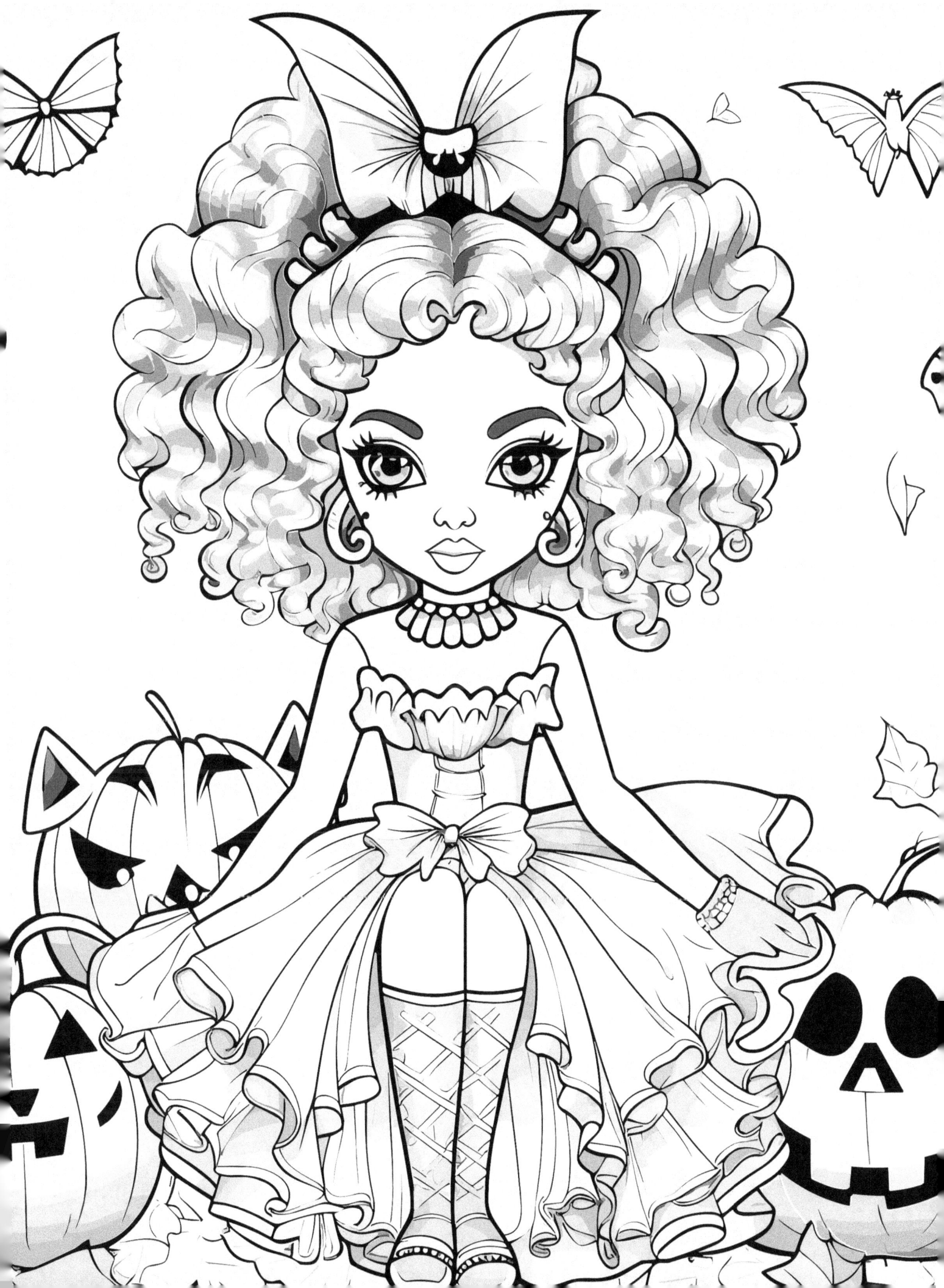

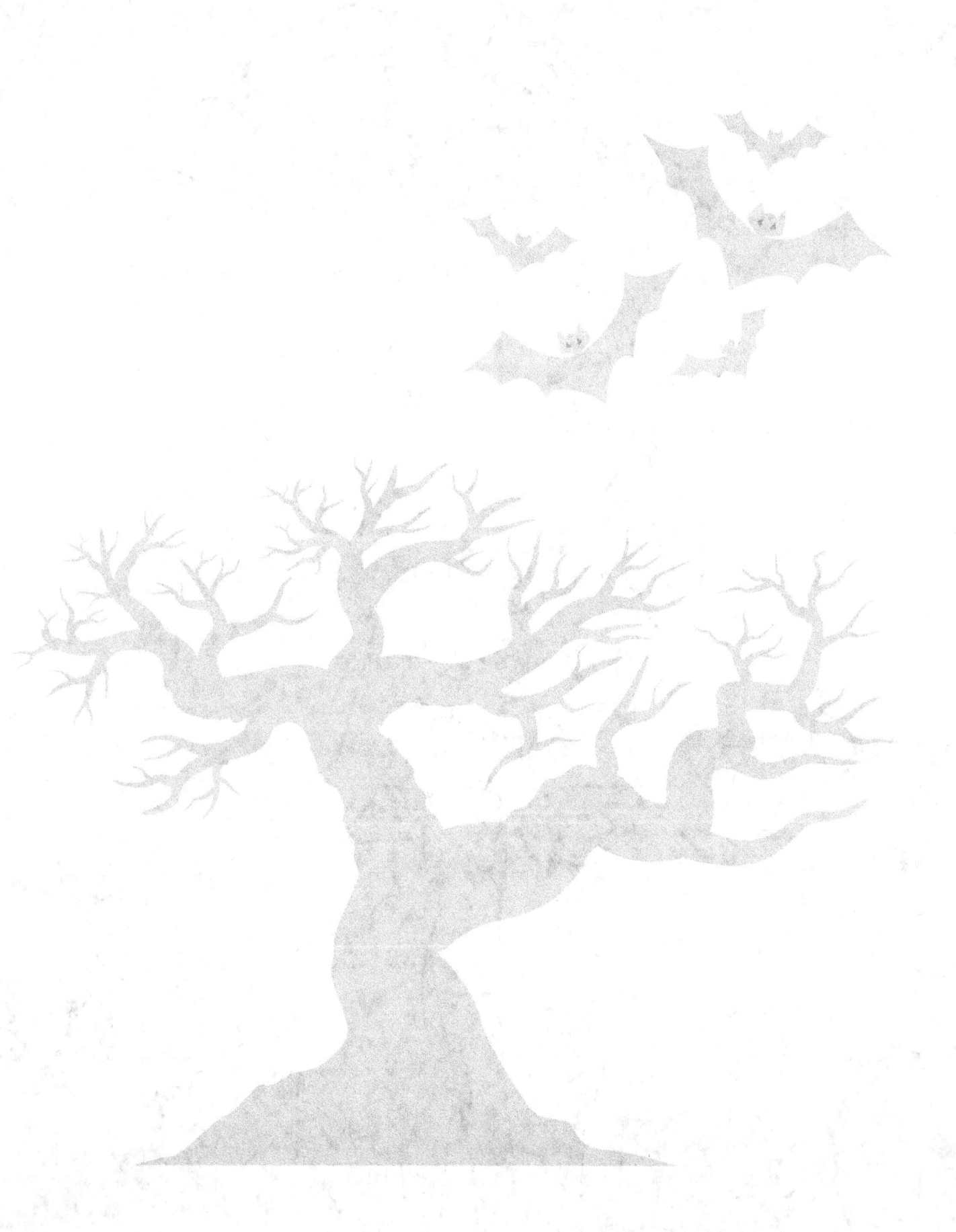

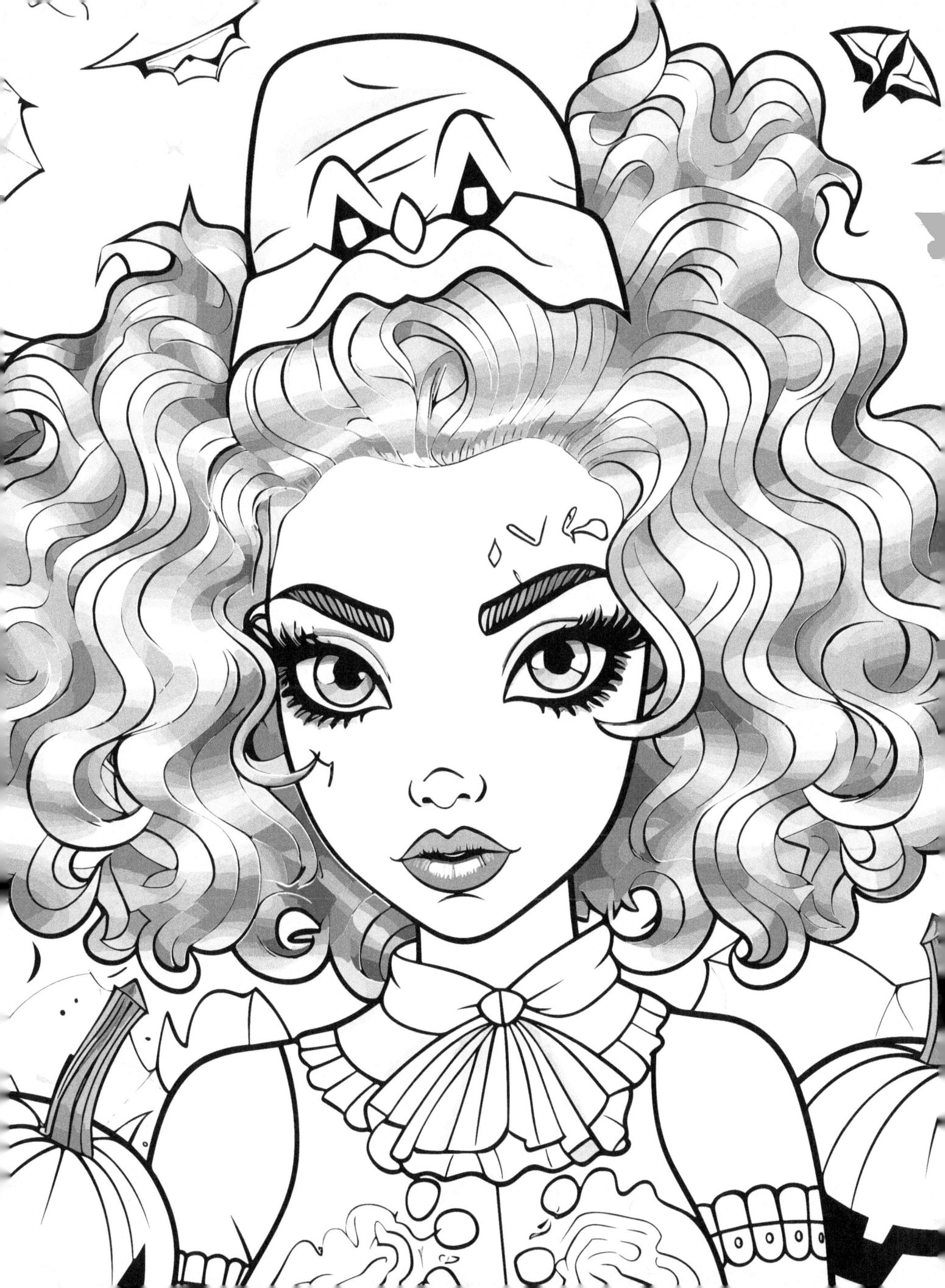

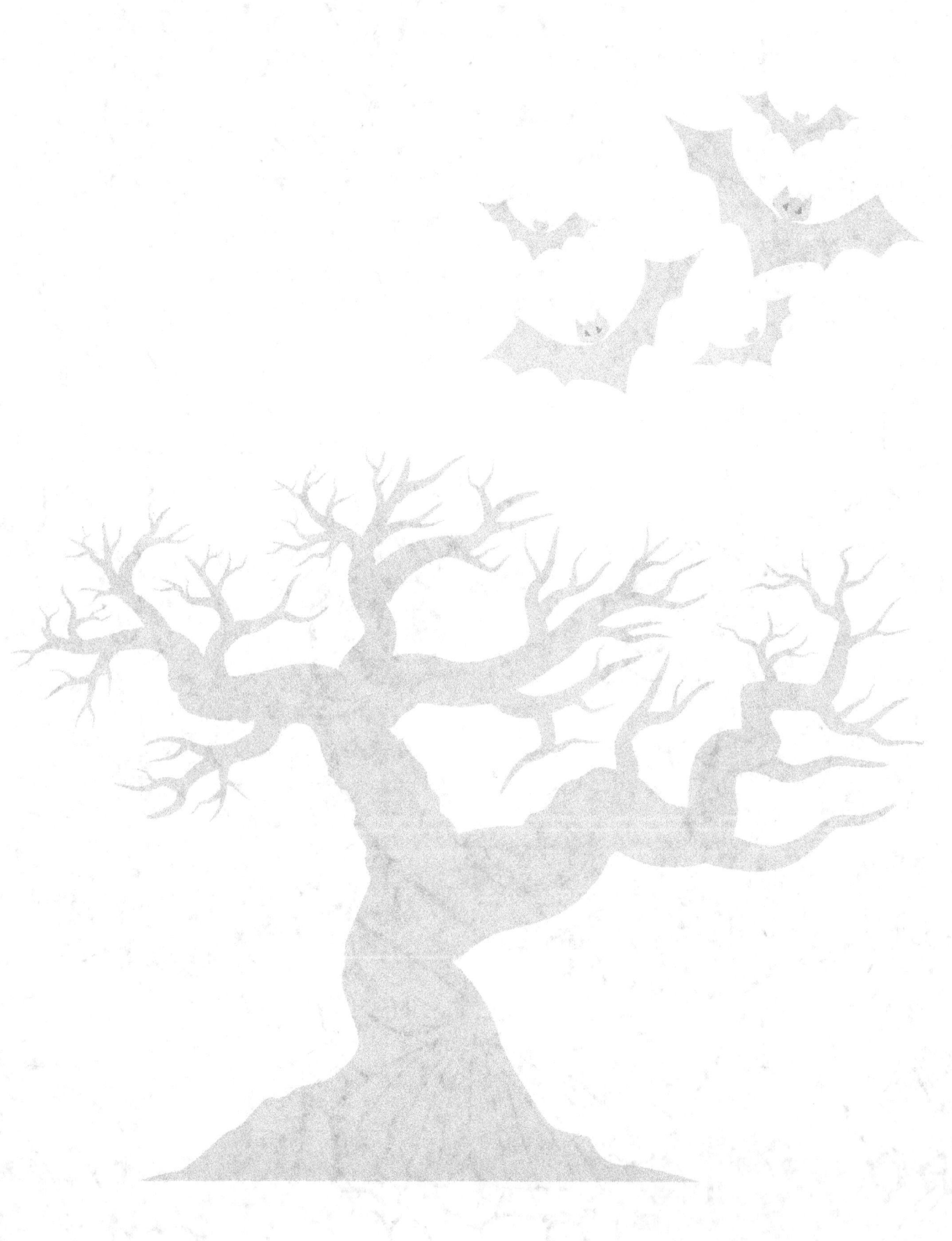

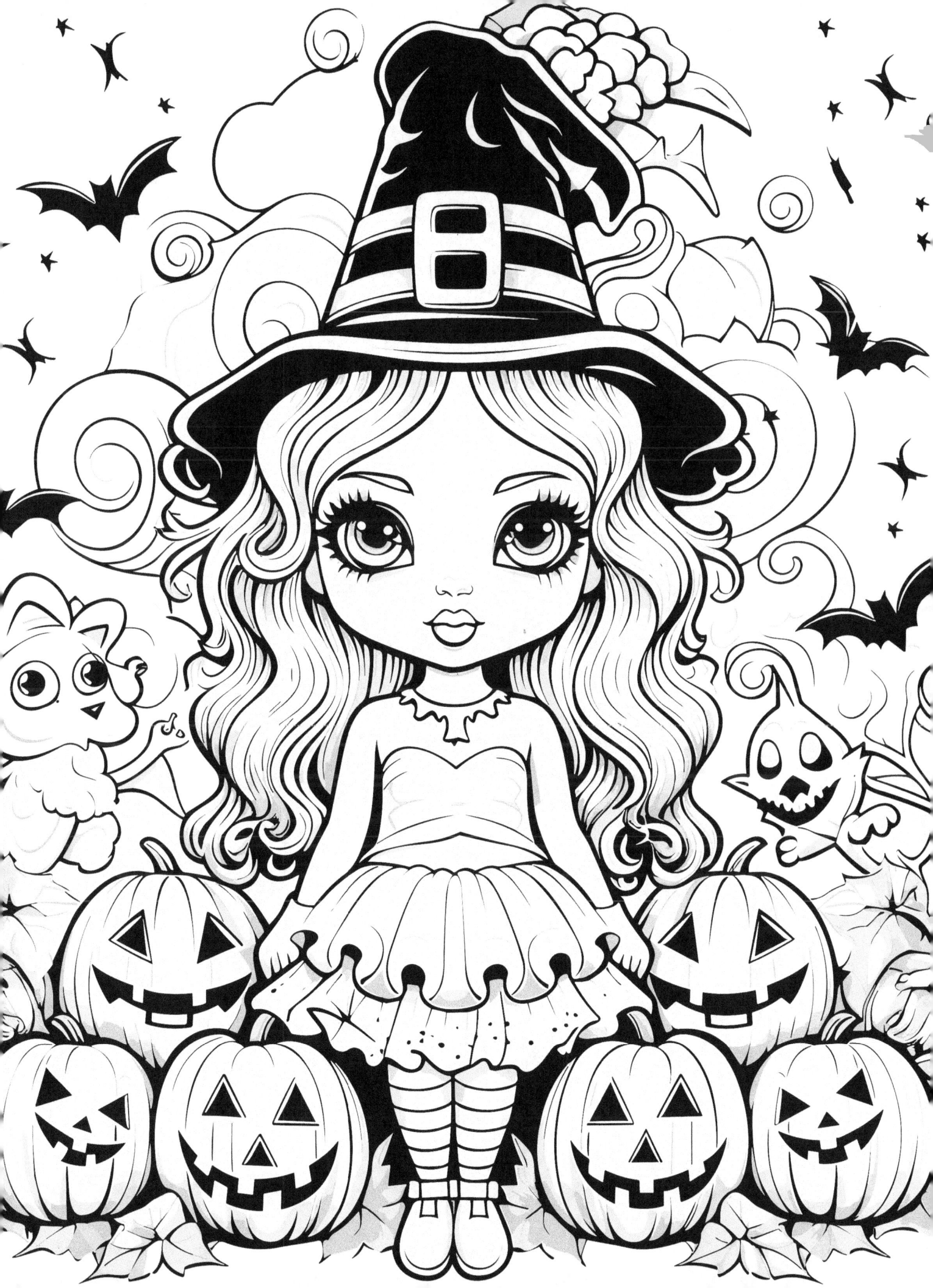

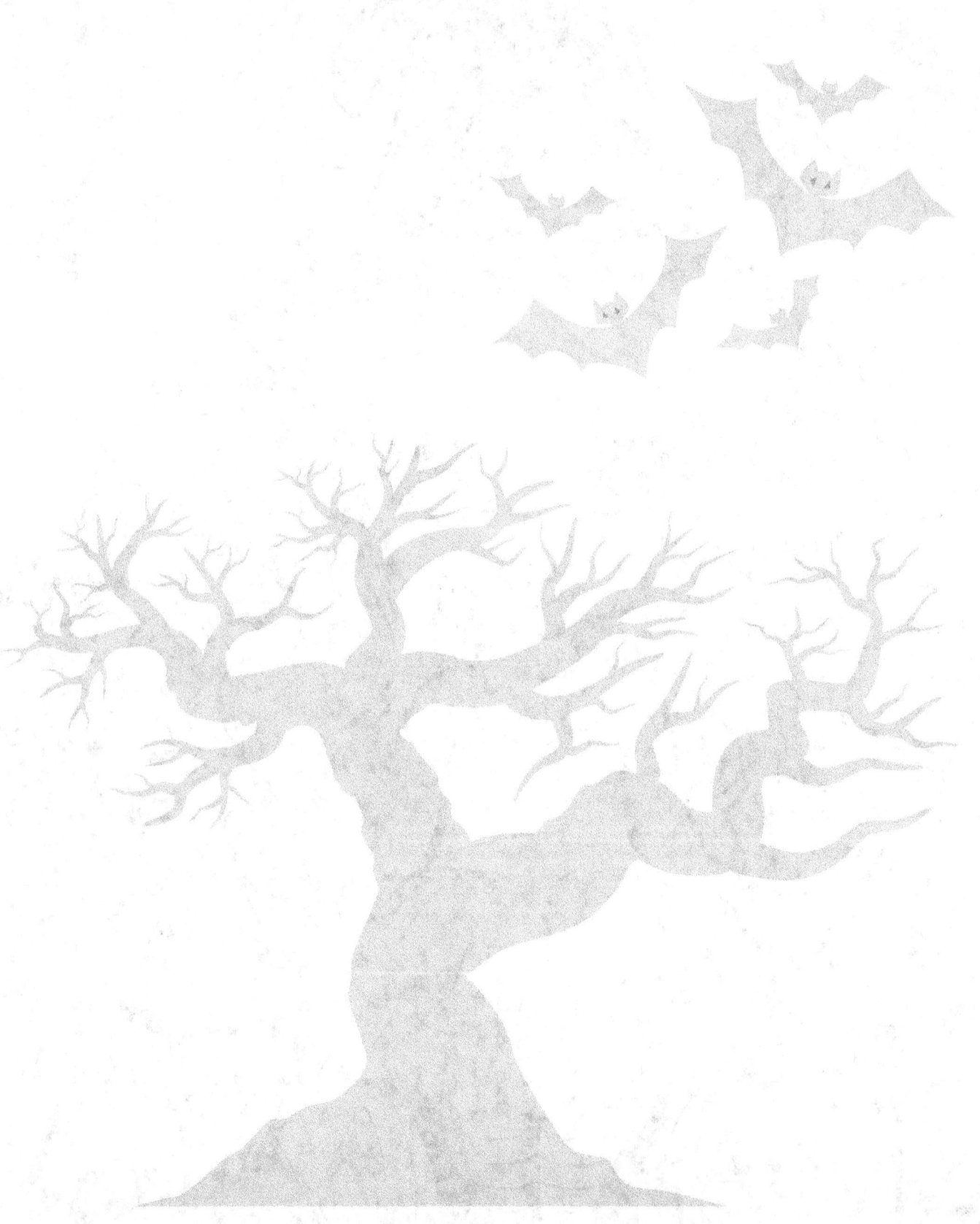

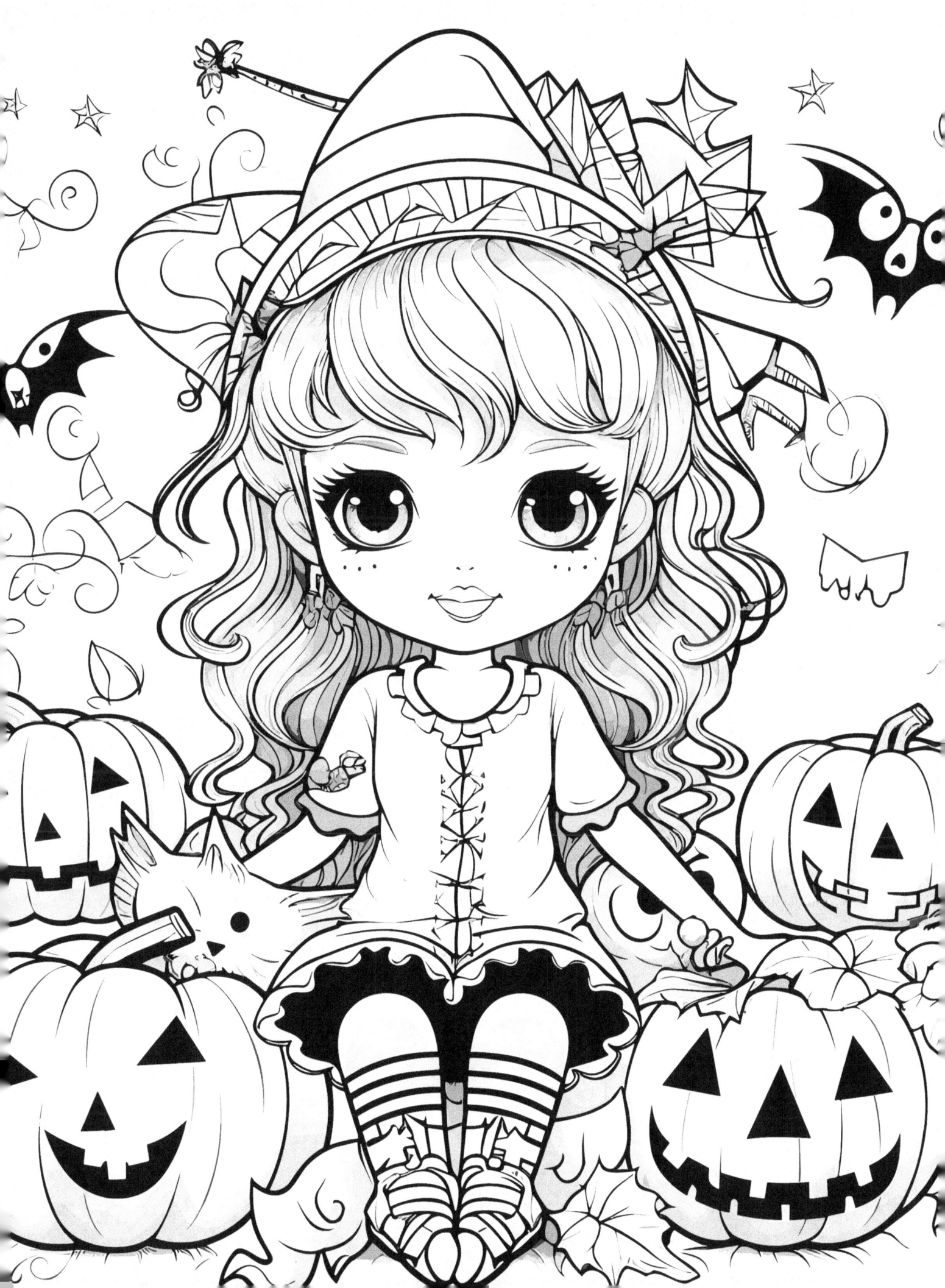

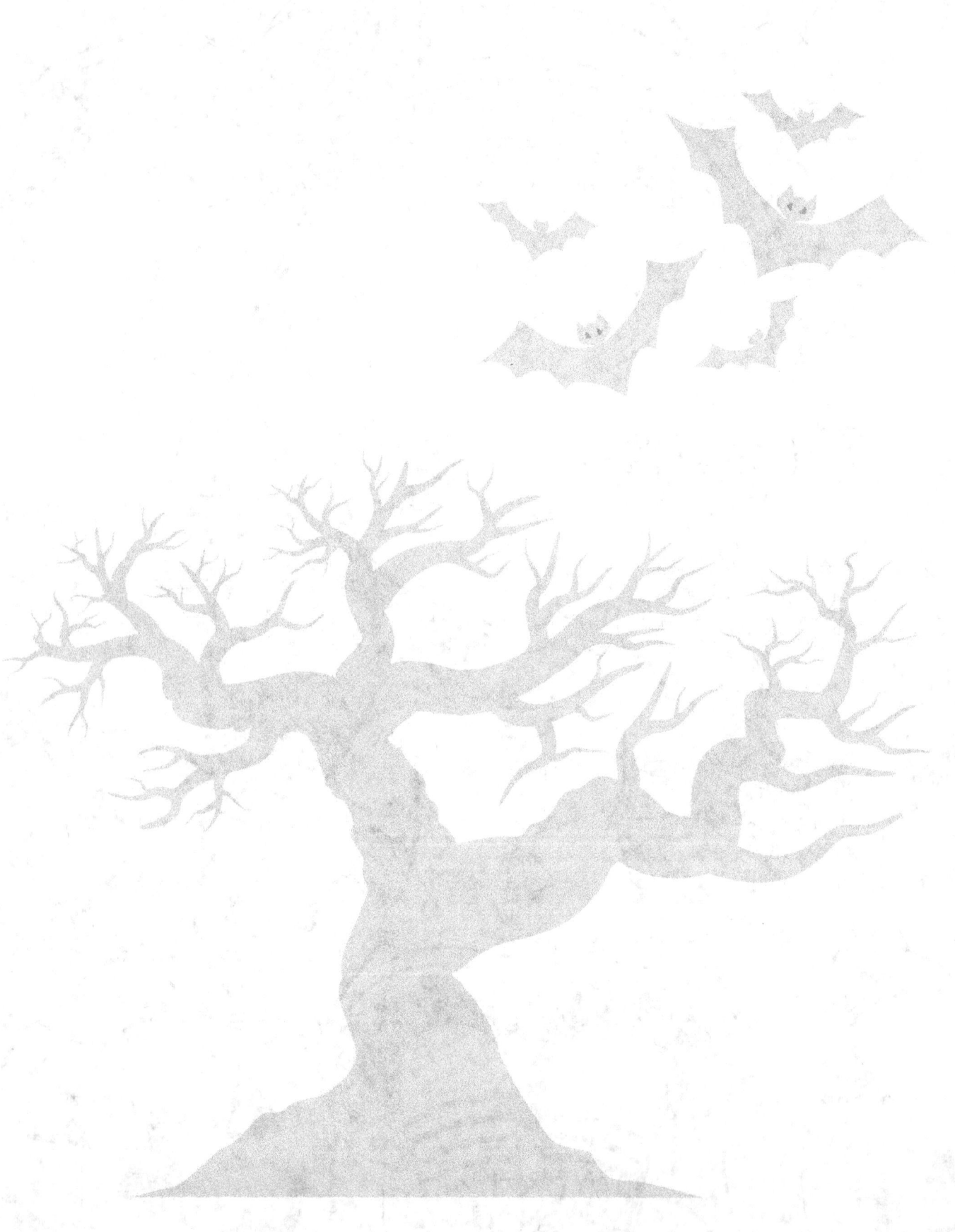

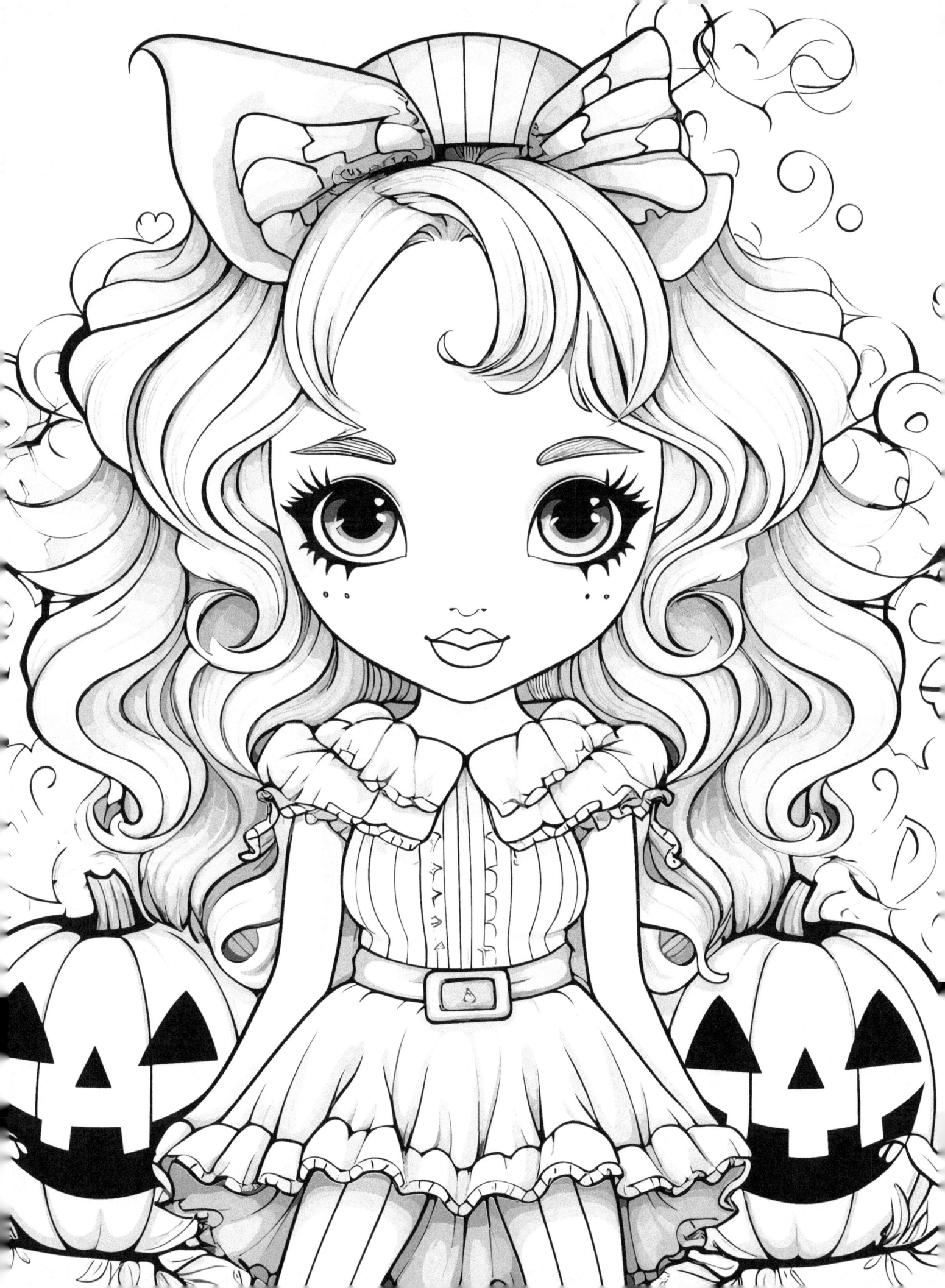

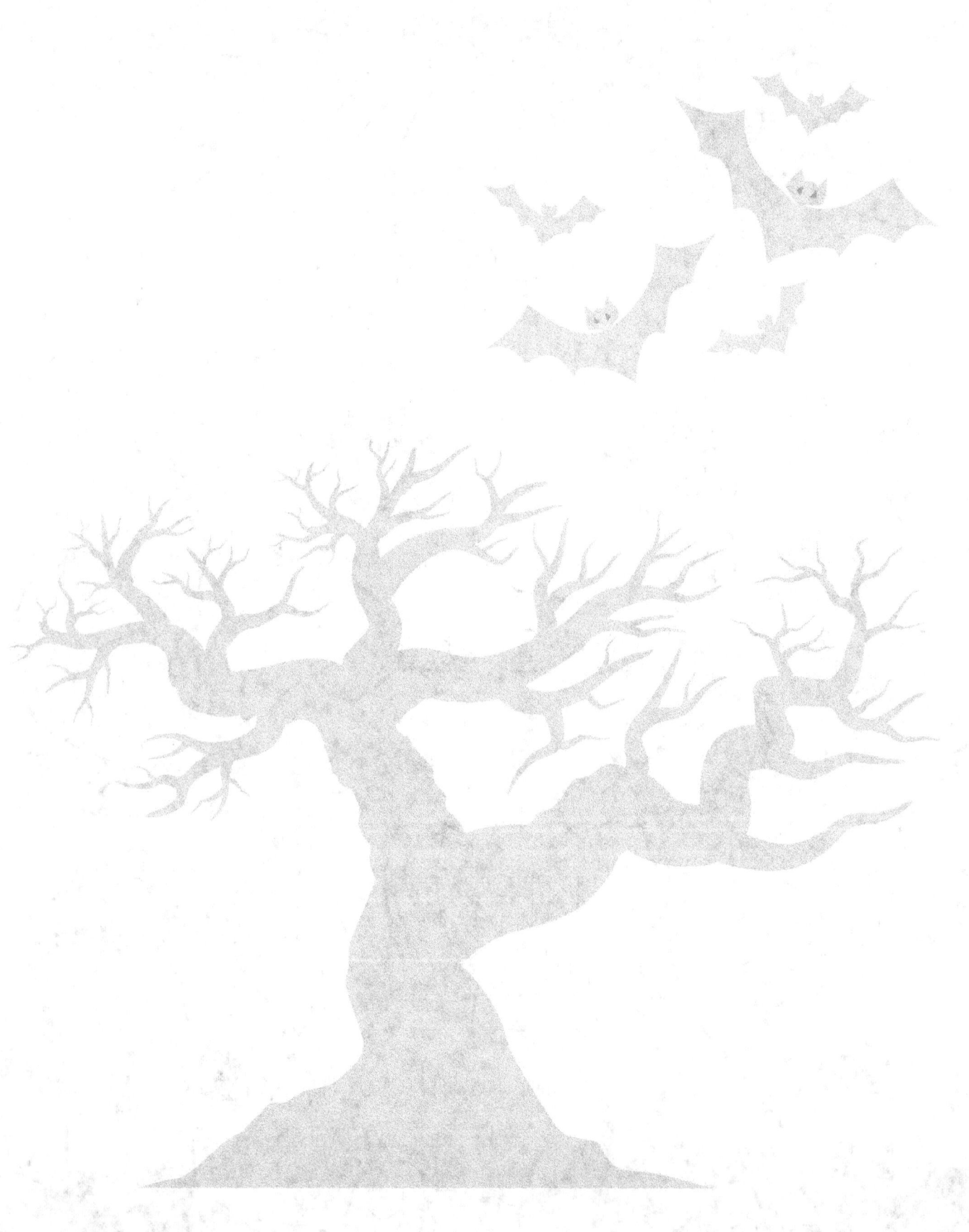

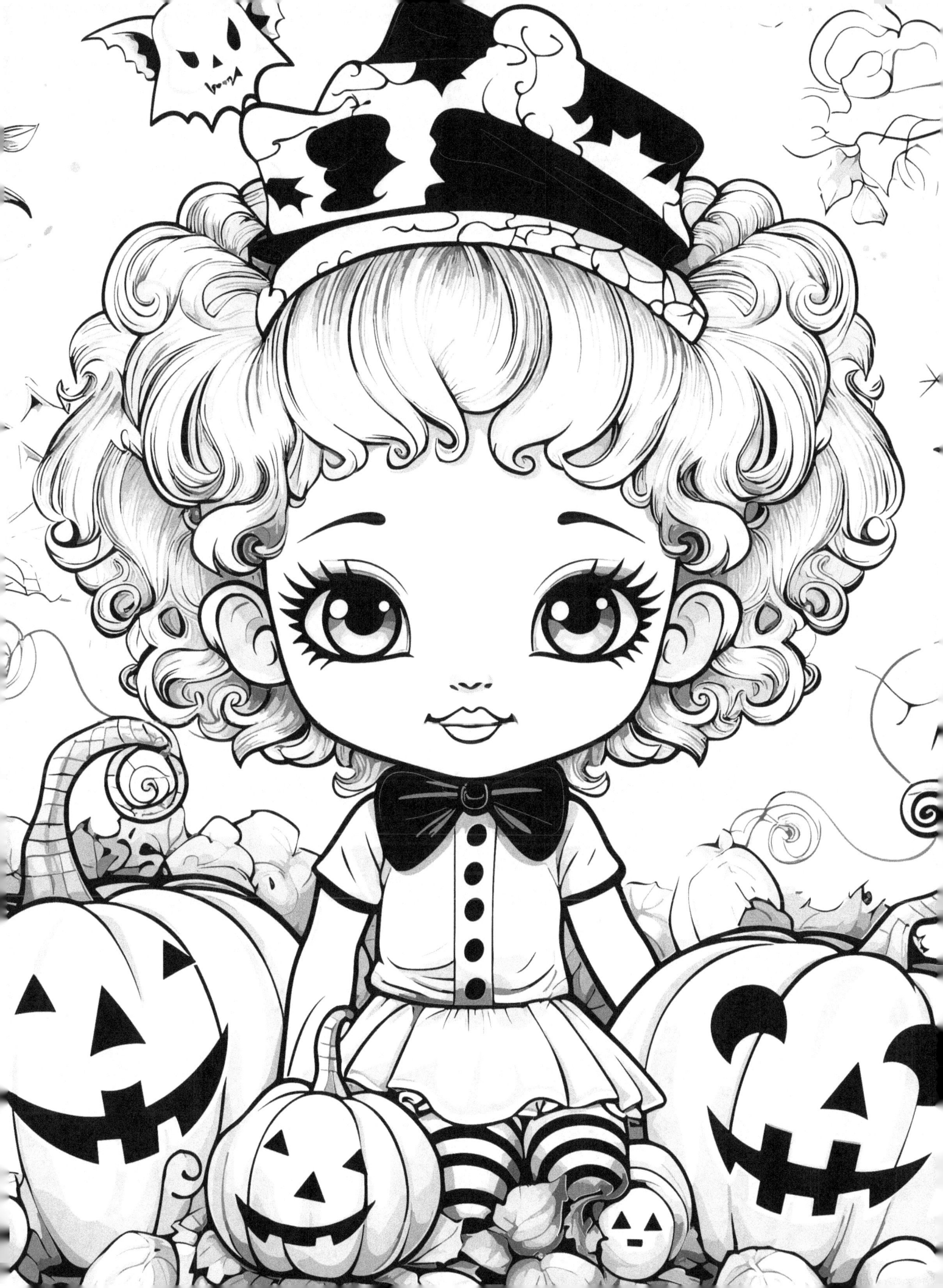

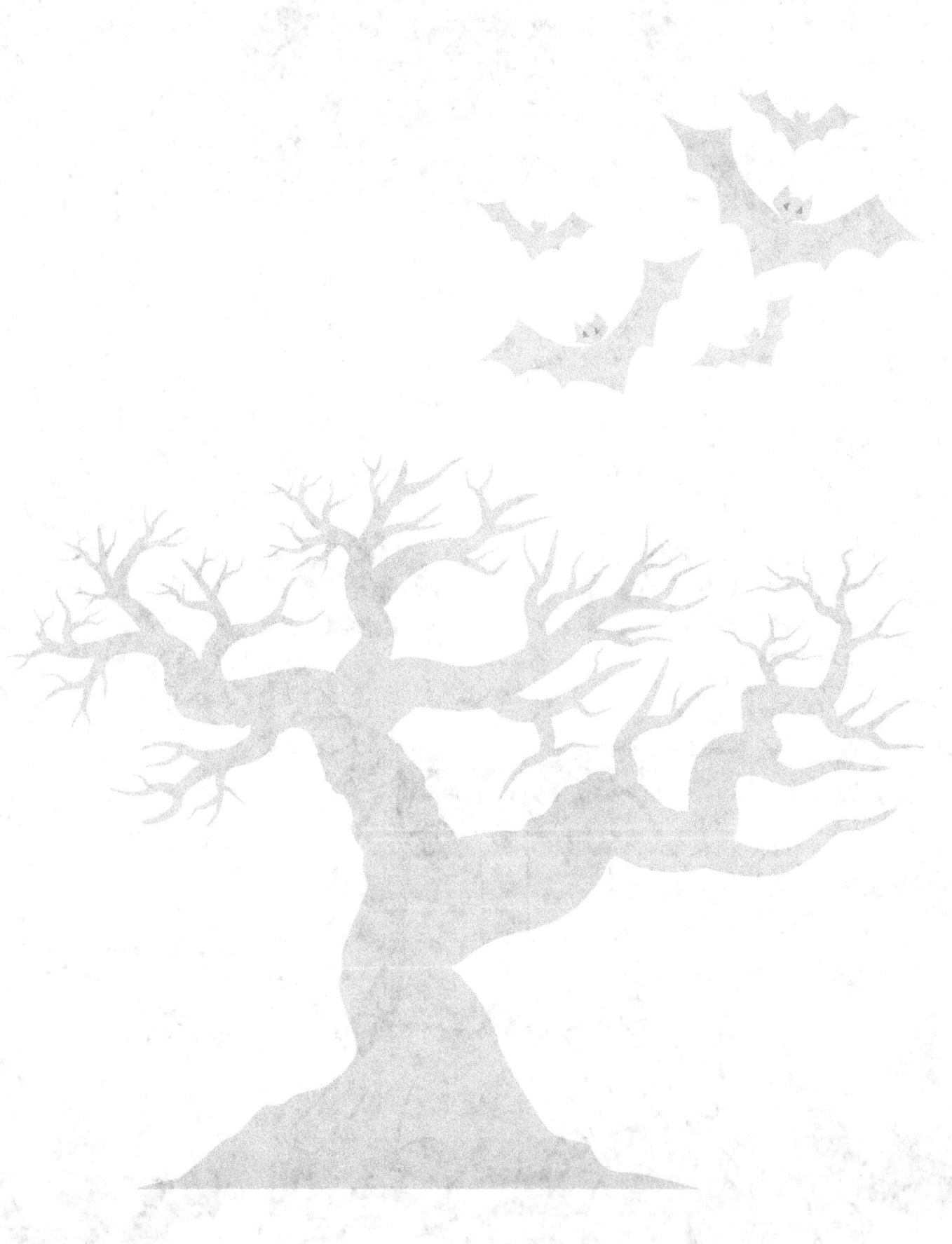

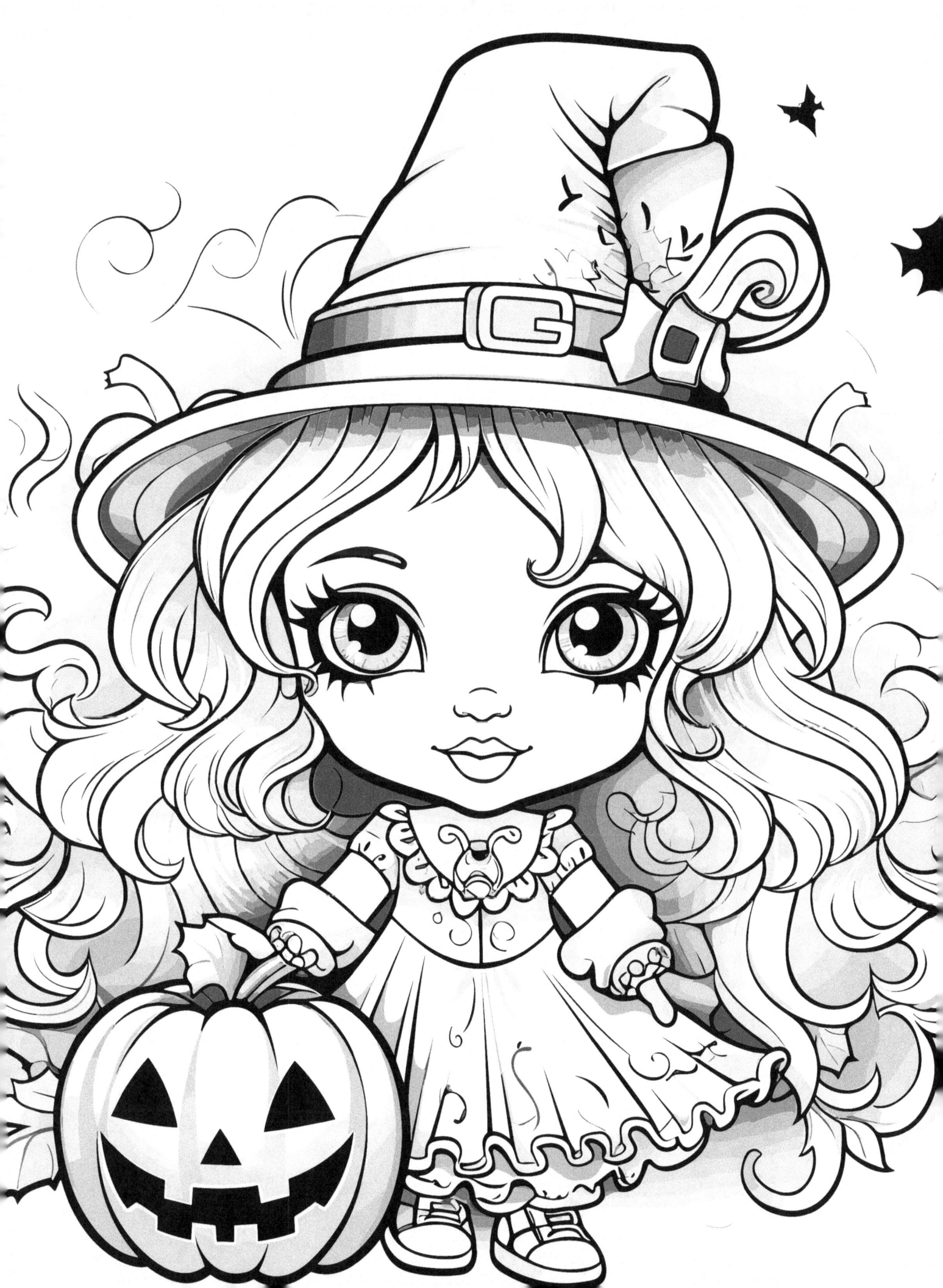

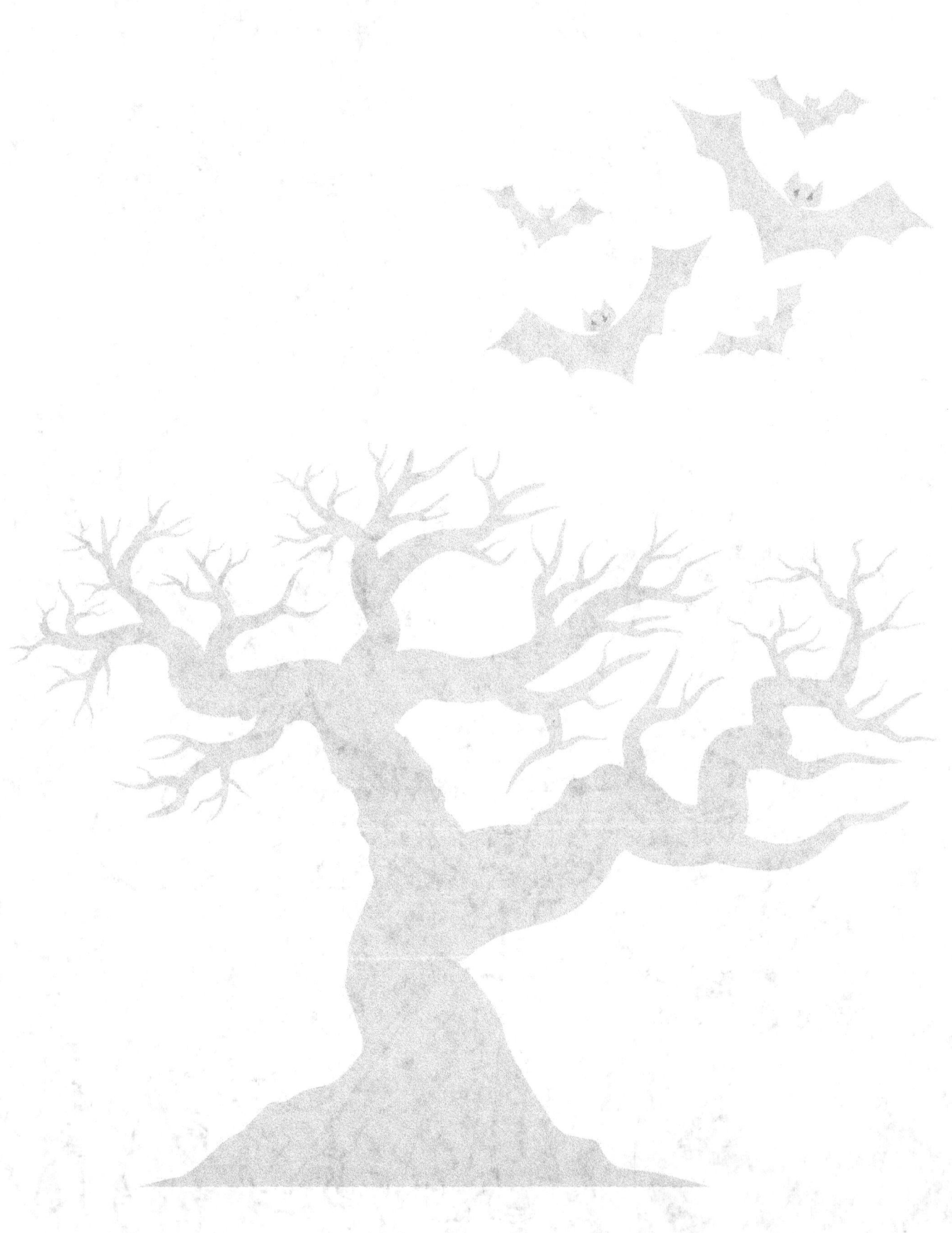

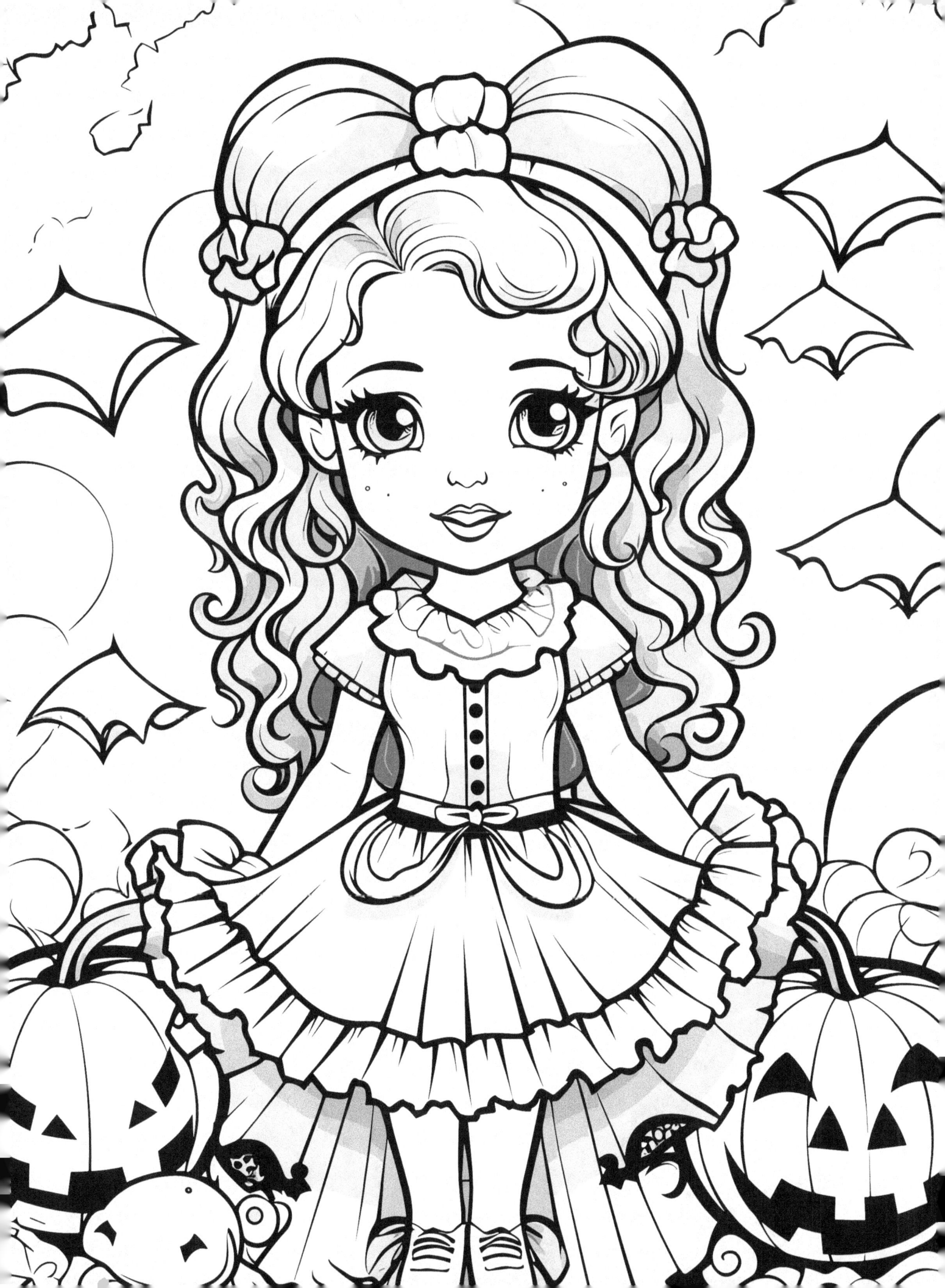

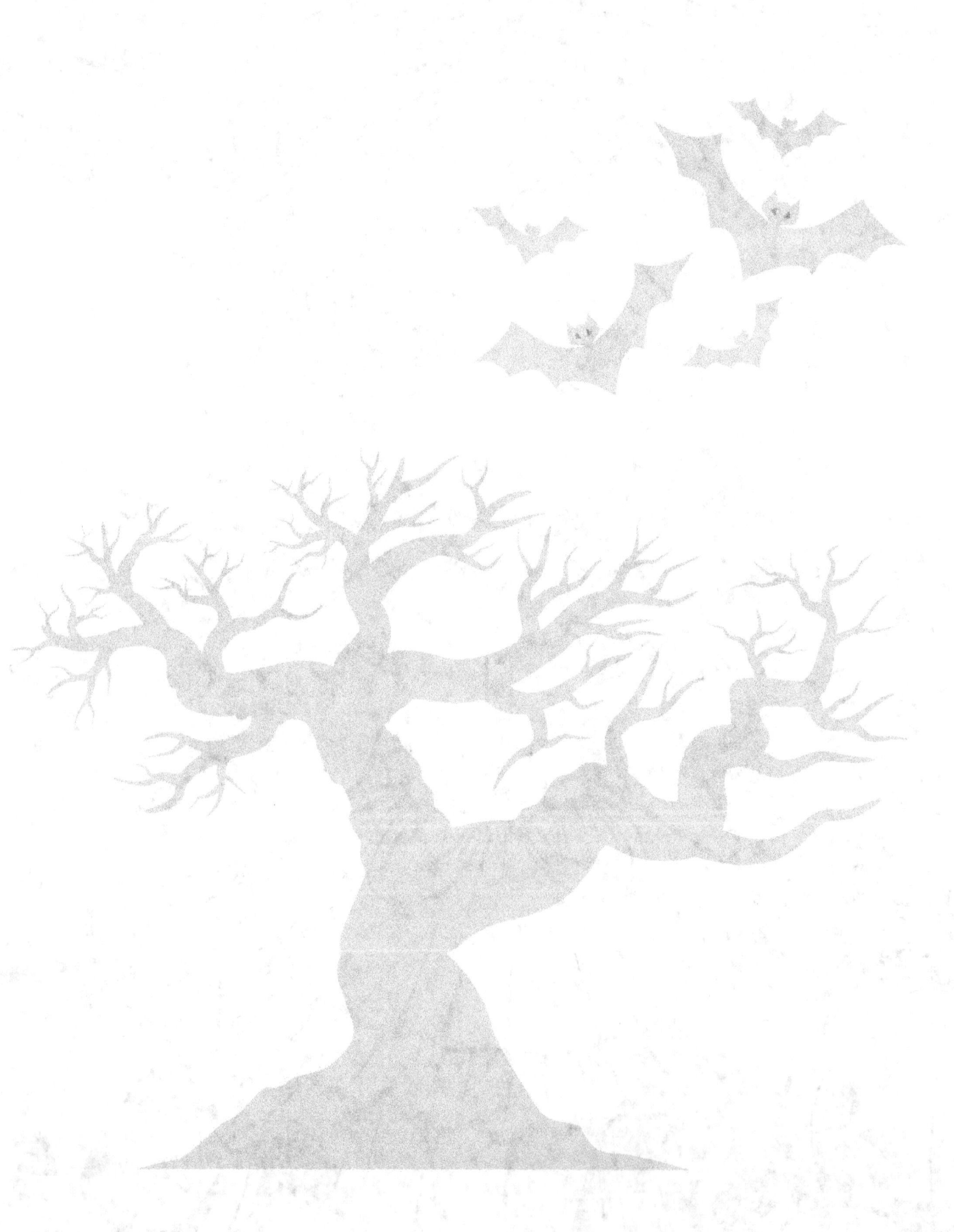

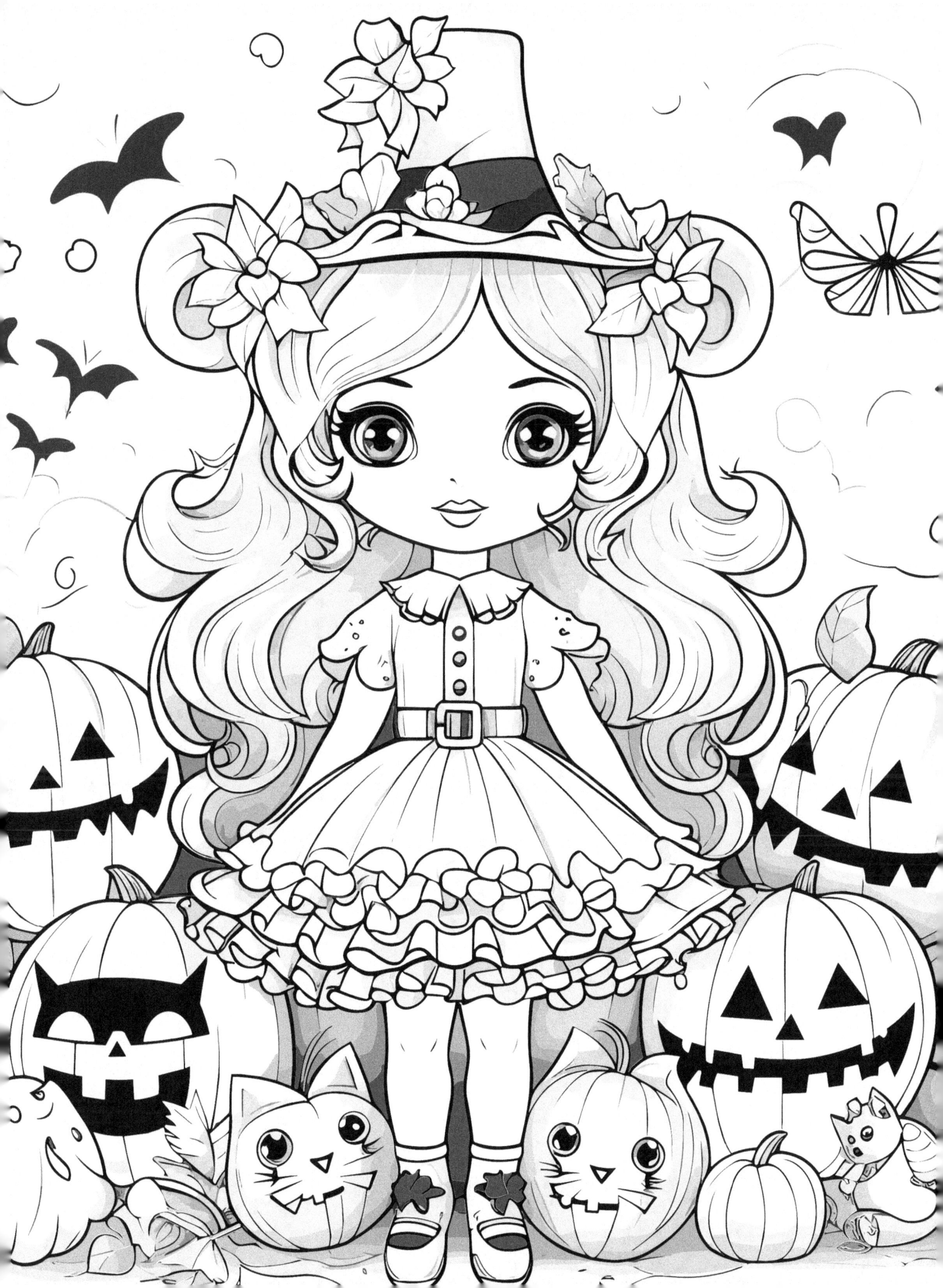

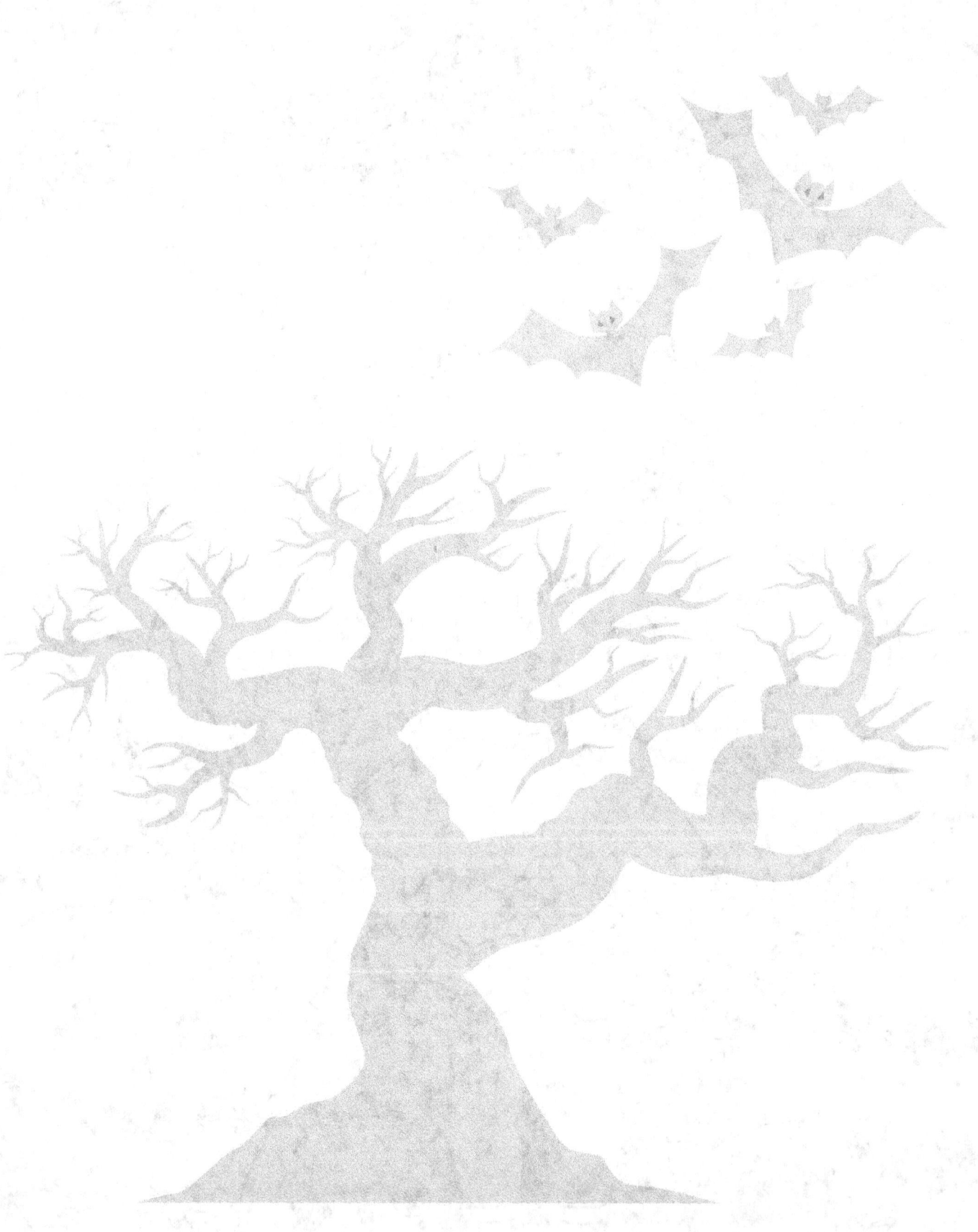

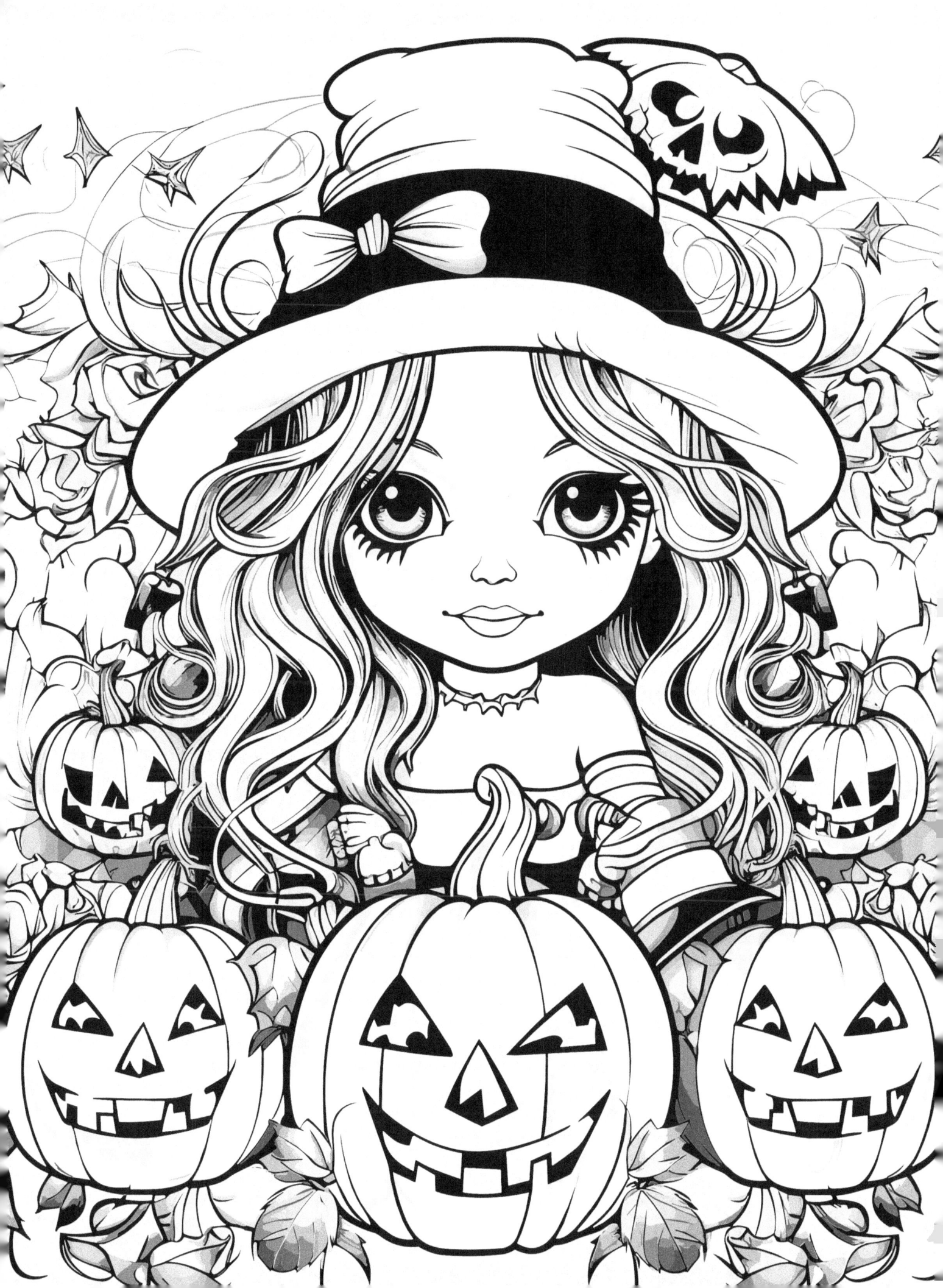

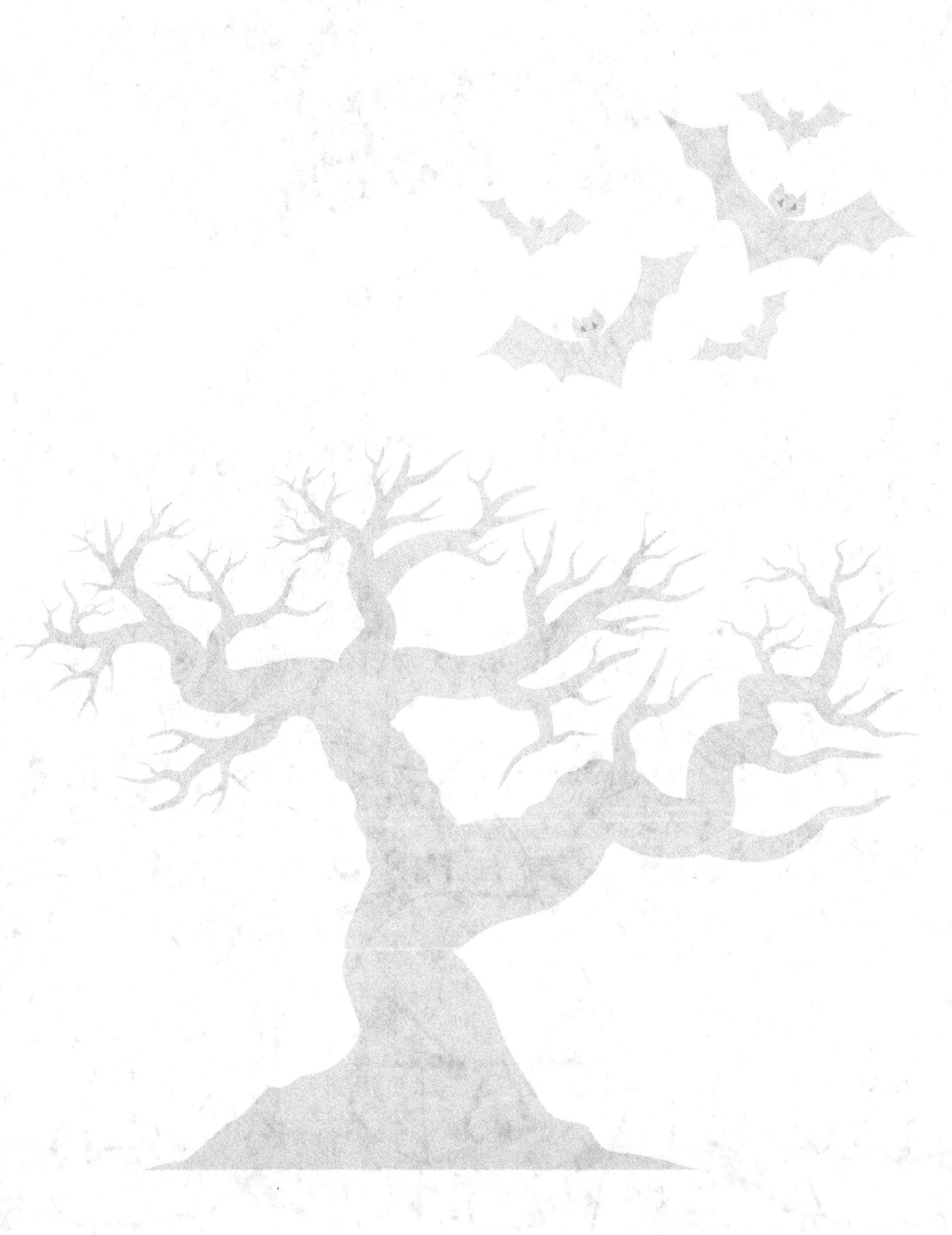

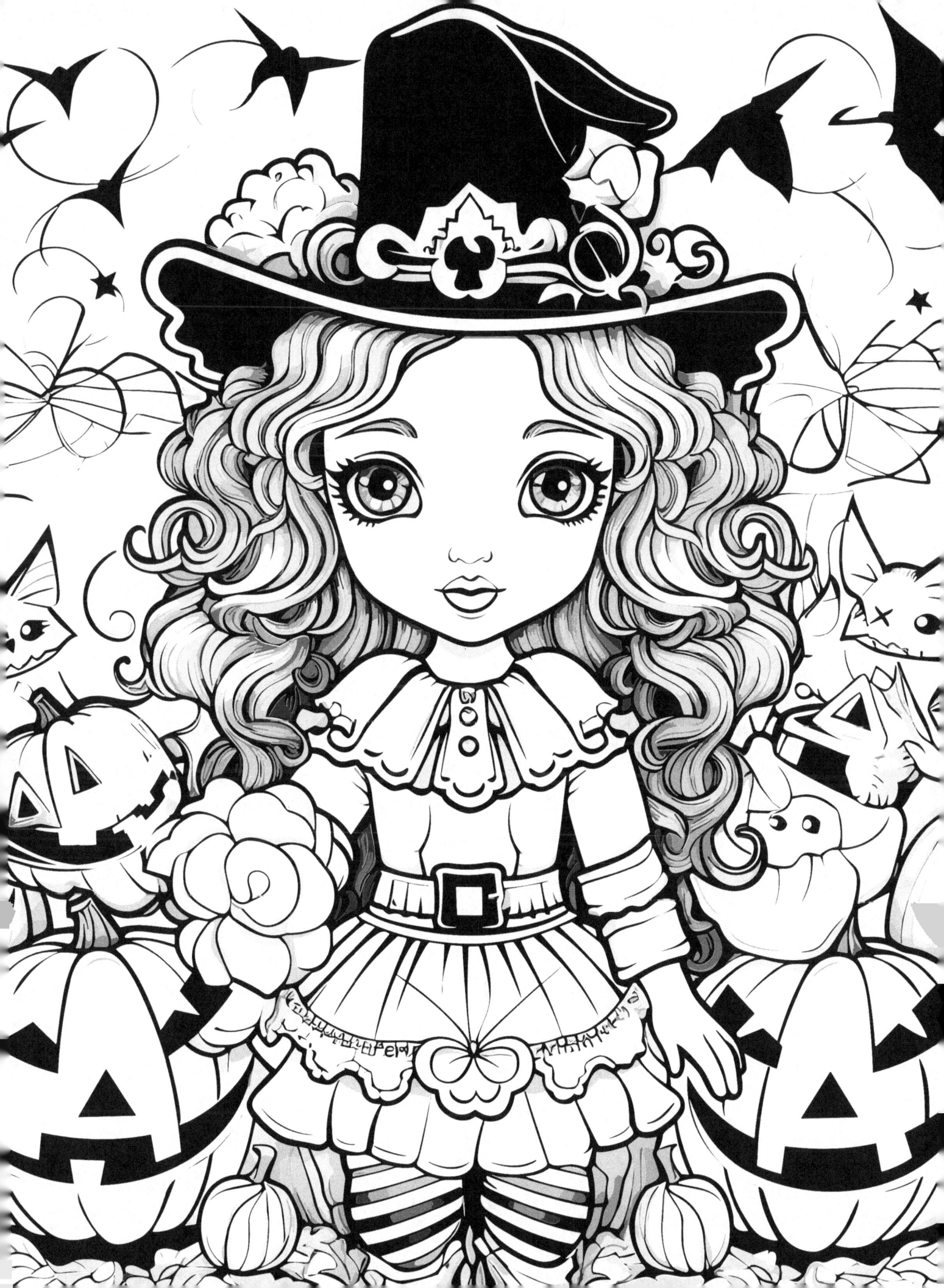

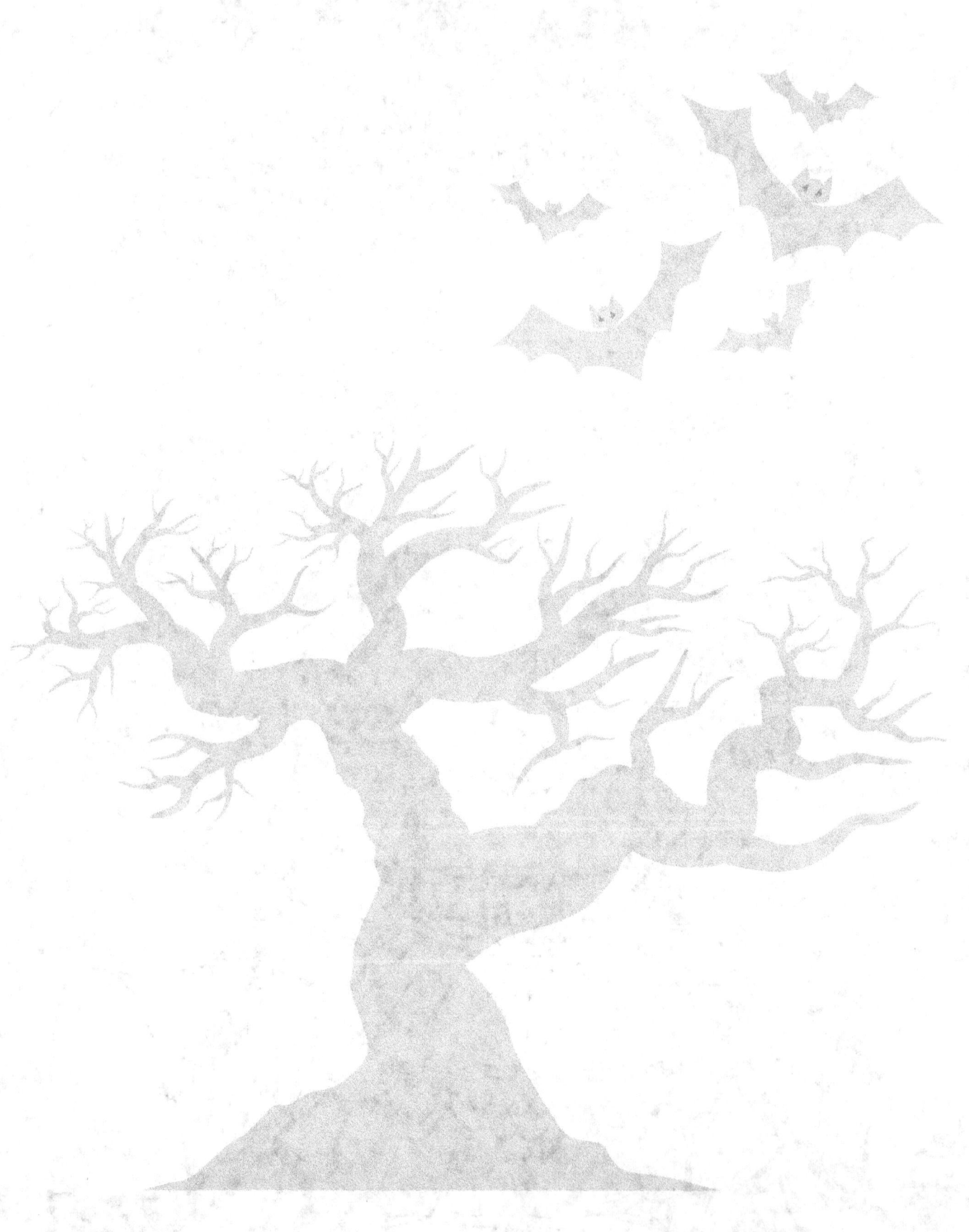

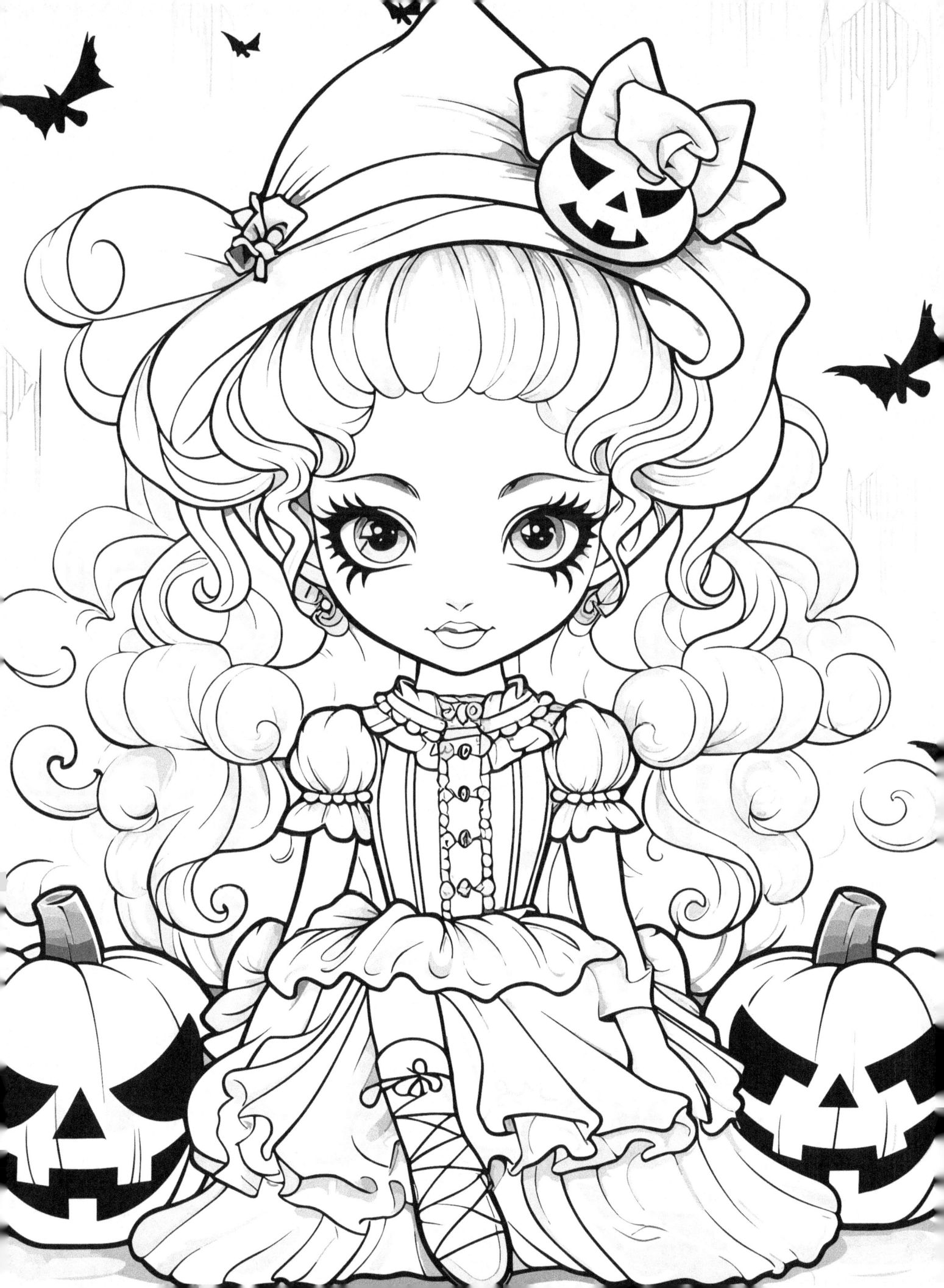

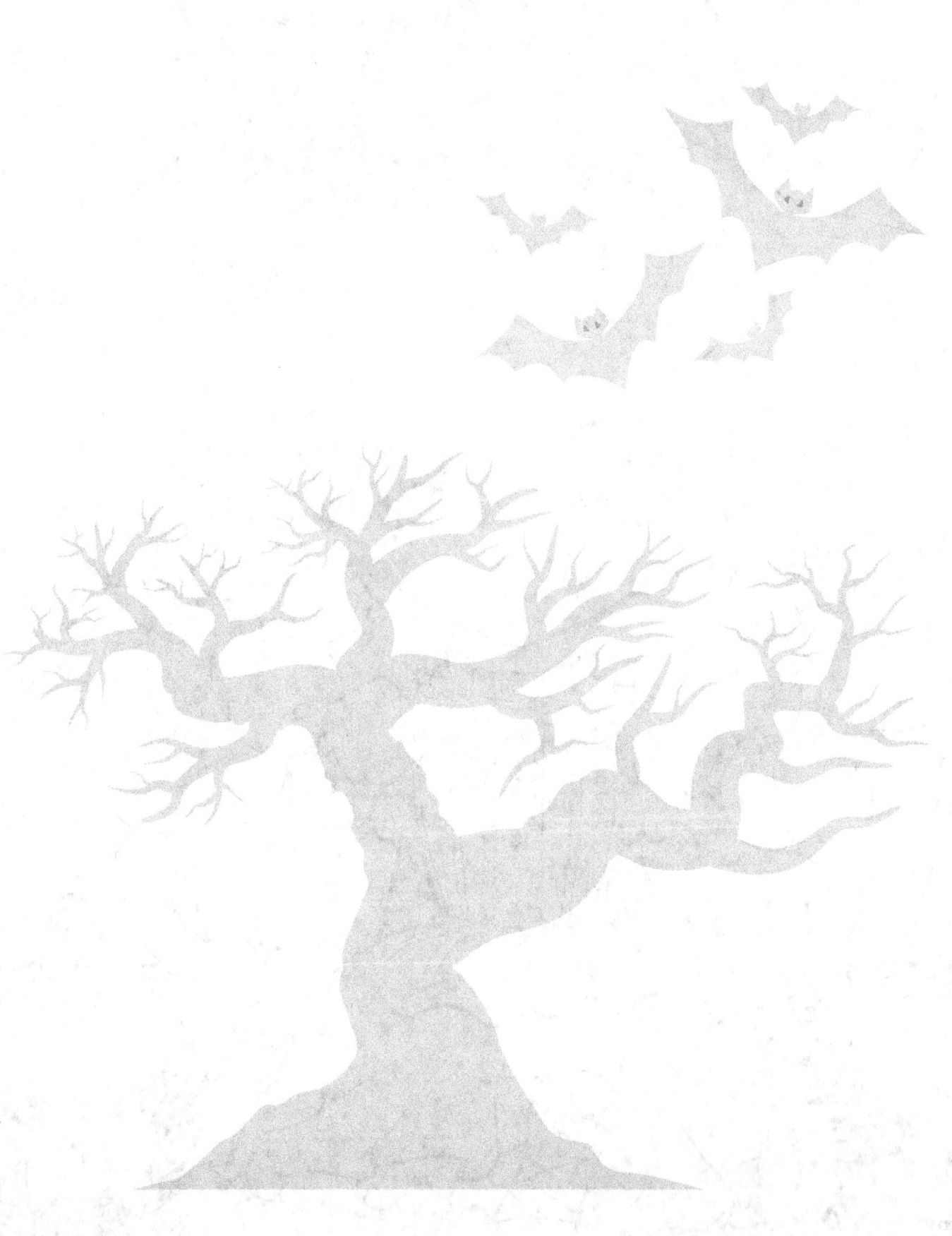

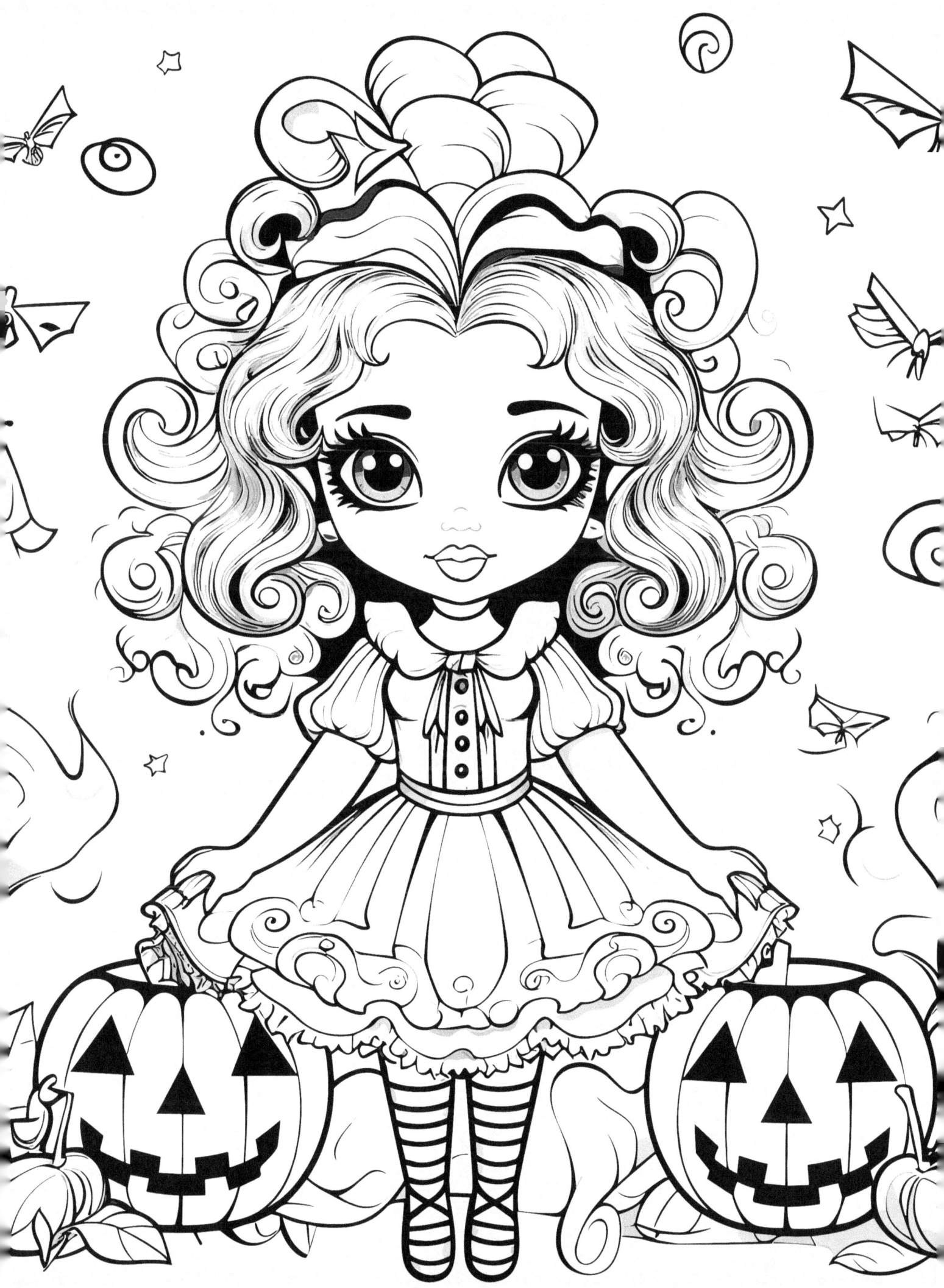

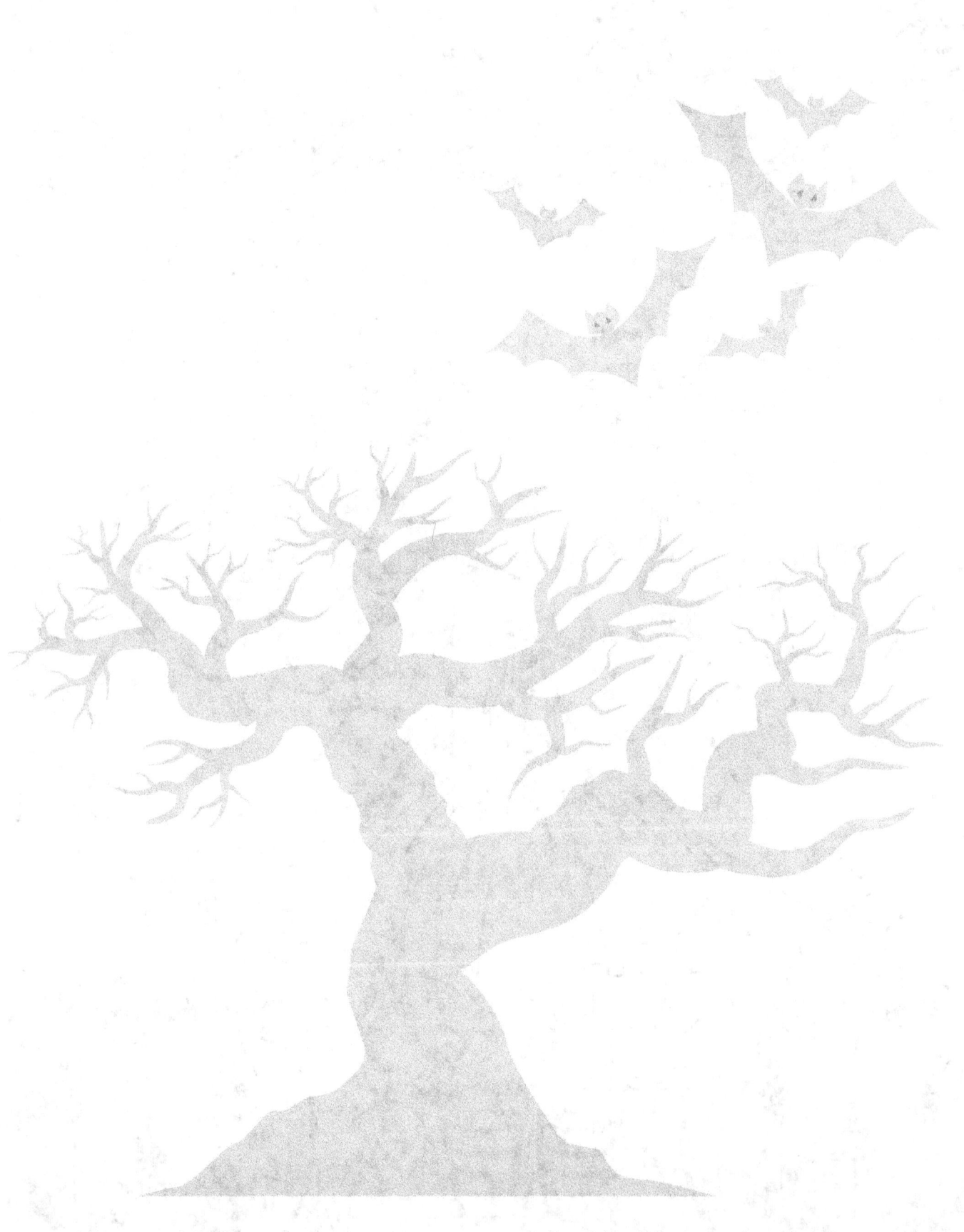

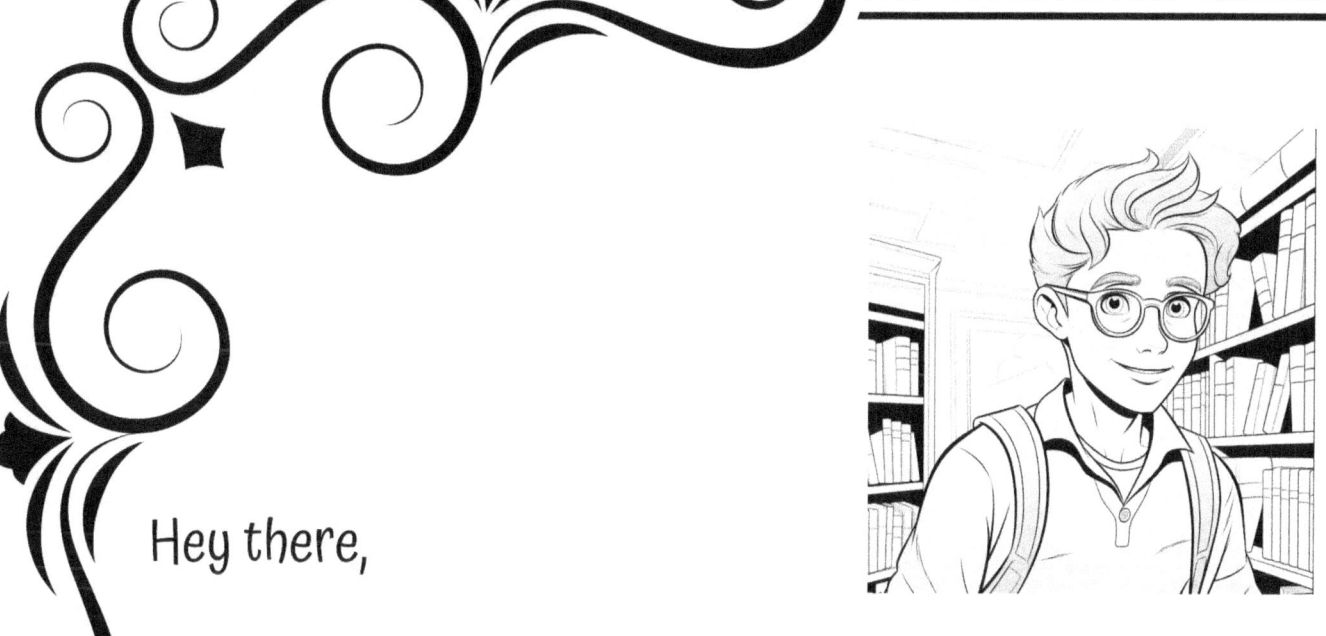

Hey there,

I'm Luís Stabile - the creative force behind "Tiny Divas Coloring Book Halloween Edition." My passion for eerie art and spine-tingling tales led me to conjure a coloring book that transcends the ordinary. With 40 bewitching divas eagerly awaiting your spectral shades, I'm thrilled to guide you on a journey where the spooky imagination knows no bounds. So, grab your broomstick, and let's brew up some enchanting colors together!

Warmly,

Luís Stabile

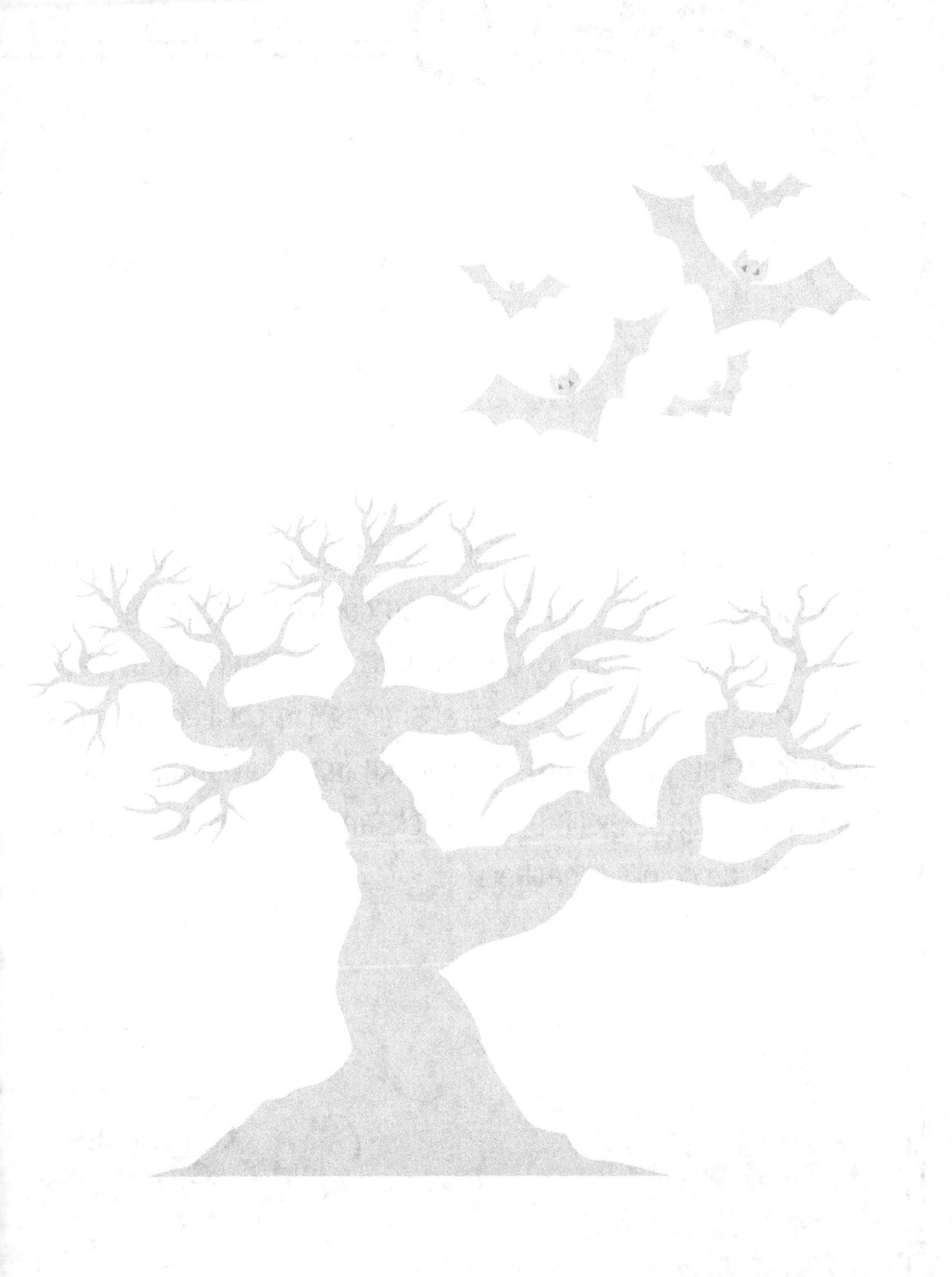